SEPT 5. 2010

THANK YOU,

THOMAS,

FOR YOUR PART IN THIS
MINISTRY! I PRAISE GOD FOR
YOU AND YOUR FAMILY. MAY
HE KEEP YOU STRONG AND
FOCUSED FOR HIM.

PSALM 1

The Amazing Way *to*

Complete Success
Lasting Wealth
Total Health
Great Joy

the testimony of
Bill Gothard, Ph.D.

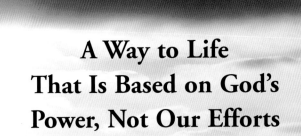

A Way to Life
That Is Based on God's
Power, Not Our Efforts

Published by the Institute in Basic Life Principles, Inc.

100087, First Printing 4/10

All Scripture verses are quoted from the King James Version of the Bible
unless otherwise noted. All emphasis added.

Images courtesy of Barak Lundberg, Britton Felber, Elizabeth Zellon, Harvey Henkelmann,
James Staddon, Mandy Novotny, Mark Czerniec, Robert Staddon, and Sara Quinnett.
Duggar family portrait by Scott Enlow. Illustration on page 10 by Ron Adair.
Bible images from Bible Pictures, courtesy of www.SolveFamilyProblems.com.

Box One
Oak Brook, IL 60522-3001
Tel: 630-323-9800 Fax: 630-323-7271
www.iblp.org

CONTENTS

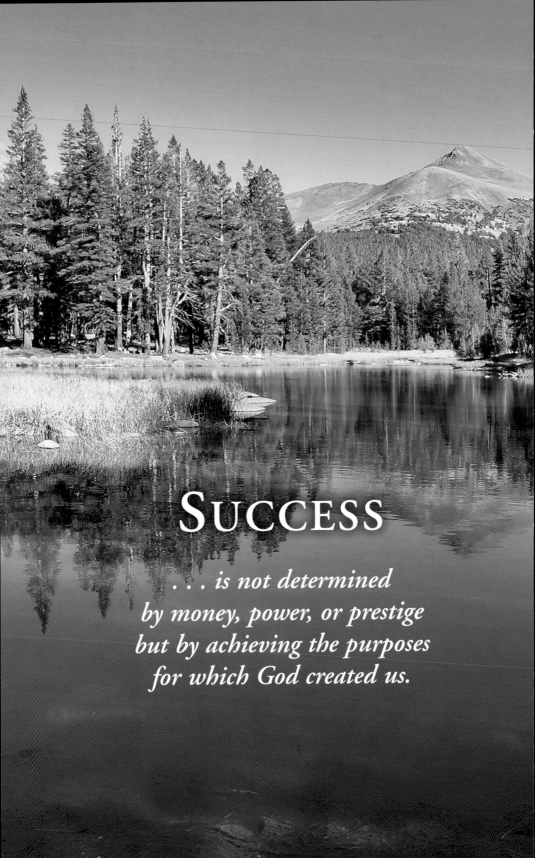

SUCCESS

*. . . is not determined
by money, power, or prestige
but by achieving the purposes
for which God created us.*

1

The Way to
COMPLETE SUCCESS:
Meditate on God's Truth!

To say that I "struggled" in school would be an understatement! I flunked the first grade and passed the next seven grades "on probation."

I will never forget the creative way by which my first grade teacher informed me that I had flunked. She

The Ogden Avenue School in LaGrange affirmed my lack of scholastic abilities.

called me out of the classroom into the hallway. There stood my mother! The teacher leaned over and enthusiastically said to me, "Billy, how would you like to be a leader in first grade, next year?" That sounded like a good idea, because I certainly had not been a leader that year—unless the competition was in earning poor grades!

The problem was that at the end of my second year in first grade, she had the same offer for me! Reluctantly I was passed to the second grade, but only if I would take summer classes in reading and improve my grades.

My mother was summoned to school by my distraught teacher.

5

A high school picture of my older sister, Anne, who has motivated me to do right throughout my life.

My second-oldest sister, Laura, who is now a great-grandmother and is also my valuable secretary.

Lyons Township High School—the place where I put into practice the secret of success

As I approached high school, my two older sisters groaned. I asked them what was wrong with them, and one of them replied, "Next year, you will be coming to high school—if you make it—and we will be known as the sisters of 'the dumbbell'!" With that motivation, I purposed to get good grades!

I spent up to five or six hours each night on homework. However, no matter how hard I tried, my grades were only average or below. Then one day a Godly older friend of our family, Mrs. Maley, asked me, "Bill, would you like to really be successful in your life?" I replied, "Yes, I would!" She said, "You can do it by memorizing large portions of Scripture."

She gave me a book that contained many passages of Scripture, and every week I would quote them to her and explain how I had tried to apply them in my life. Unknowingly, I was not only memorizing but also meditating on Scripture, which means that I was learning and applying God's Word in my life daily.

God's Word states that meditation on Scripture, followed by obedience, will result in prosperity. This is what the Lord spoke to His servant Joshua: "This book of the law shall not depart out of thy mouth; but thou shalt meditate therein day and night, that thou mayest observe to do according to all that is written therein: for then thou shalt make thy way prosperous, and then thou shalt have good success" (Joshua 1:8).

At the end of the next semester, I got my report card. The grades were A– average with no extra time spent on homework!

I continued meditating on Scripture through the rest of my high school years, graduated as a member of the National Honor Society, and even was offered a partial scholarship to Harvard University.

Wheaton College and Graduate School

During my years at Wheaton College and Wheaton Graduate School, my grades were earned in direct proportion to how faithful I was at meditating on Scripture.

Not only did my grades go up, but I became successful in everything I did. I entered a national science contest and won a top award with a project on metallography. I entered a Scripture Press book-writing contest and won an award. My art teacher entered an art project I had made in her class in a national art contest. Not only was it given a high award, but it was also exhibited in cities around the nation!

When the LaGrange Art Club heard about my work, they gave me a scholarship to attend a summer course at the Chicago Art Institute. During that summer, I took a course in layout and design, and it has been a great benefit to me over the years.

During his years at Wheaton College, Billy Graham preached on a local radio program.

I really felt that I had an unfair advantage over the other contestants because of my understanding of God's promise to those who meditate on His Law day and night.

There were many nights when I put myself to sleep by quoting Psalm 1: "Blessed is the man that walketh not in the counsel of the ungodly, nor standeth in the way of sinners, nor sitteth in the seat of the scornful. But his delight is in the law of the LORD; and in his law doth he meditate day and night. . . . And whatsoever he doeth shall prosper." Then, I would pray, "Lord, I will meditate to experience your blessing."

When my father heard Billy Graham preach the Gospel over the radio, my father accepted Christ as his Savior.

Affectionately known as the "Old Lighthouse," the Pacific Garden Mission of Chicago has been a location for life transformations for more than one hundred years. An unexpected life-changing event happened to me at this mission.

During high school, I viewed life as a race against time. I wanted to set aside anything that would not help me reach my goals. So I developed this philosophy:

"Others may. I cannot."

The Power of Personal Vows!

The more that I meditated on Scripture, the more I was motivated to make vows as an expression of my love for God so that I would not violate His Word.

A Vow to Not Go to Movies

One of my first vows was made when I was a young boy. My father took me with him to the Pacific Garden Mission in Chicago for a Saturday night meeting, which was an outreach to alcoholics.

My father had been appointed as the chairman of the mission's board of directors. During his term of office, he helped start the radio program *Unshackled*. It is currently the longest-running radio drama in the history of radio and is heard around the world.

At the close of the meeting, my father walked to the front of the auditorium to pray with some of the men. Meanwhile, I slipped out of my chair and wandered out to see the sights of Chicago.

As I went down the street, I was intrigued by what was going on. In front of one store was a mounted viewer. It promised to reveal "spectacular sights" to the person who inserted a nickel. I put in my nickel and pressed my face against the viewer. The "spectacular sights" turned out to be very disillusioning, and I felt cheated out of my nickel.

By that time, my father had realized that I was missing and had run out to the street to look for me. I heard him calling out: "Billy! Billy!" When he saw me, he ran down the street to get me. As I looked up into his grief-stricken face, he spoke words that I will never forget: "This is awful! I came down here to save these alcoholics, and I lose my own son!"

I did not think that he had lost me, but his hatred of evil had a profound effect upon me. He took my arm and walked me back to our green Chrysler for the ride home. As we drove out of the mission parking lot, I looked across the street at the gaudy, glaring lights of a theater marquee. They were advertising a "spectacular" film, and I thought to myself, "That movie is probably as disillusioning as the viewer on which I just lost my nickel."

I quietly made a vow that I never again would go into a movie theater—not even for a "good movie."

During the past sixty-plus years, that vow has been like a beacon of light. It has been tested several times—even by family members who urged me to go with them to see a Christian movie that was being shown in a local theater.

One of the many resulting benefits of this vow was the reasoning that since I had vowed to not watch godless movies in a theater, why should I watch them outside of a theater? This understanding gave me a powerful freedom to say "no" to many things that potentially could have damaged or destroyed my walk with God and my ability to work with young people.

A Vow to Not Kiss Before Marriage

My two older sisters, Anne and Laura, have exerted a profound influence on my life over the years. When I was about thirteen years old, they were having a conversation in our front parlor about a young man from our church youth group. He had dated one of their girlfriends and kissed her after the date.

The young lady became enthralled with his attention and immediately gave her heart to him. A few weeks later, he "dropped" her for another girl.

Before I entered high school, Jack Hamilton, the founder of the Bible Quizzing movement, gave me counsel that I will never forget:

"Bill, when a farmer plows a field, he must make sure that the first furrows are straight, so he lines up a post at the end of the field with a distant tree. When they are both together, he knows that he is on track. "When you get to high school, ask yourself two questions about any extracurricular activity: 'Will this count ten years from now?' and 'Will this count in eternity?'" These questions gave me much extra time to help my classmates learn about God's way of life.

I learned early in life that the disciplines exercised before marriage would result in a stronger marriage relationship.

When I am tempted to look at pornography, I remember that Jesus said that it would be more profitable to gouge out my eye than to look at a woman with lust. This blocks out the temptation. Samson failed in this area and had both eyes gouged out by his enemies.

She was crushed and soon walked away from the Lord and into a life of immorality.

As I listened to my sisters' remarks about their abhorrence of what he had done to damage her life, I made a vow that I would never kiss a girl until we were married. God has used this vow not only to keep me from kissing a girl but also to remind me to avoid taking advantage of her in any way.

On several occasions, girls have given me clear opportunities to violate my moral standards. My first response has been, "Do I want to be married to this girl for the rest of my life?" The answer was always "no." Therefore, I said to myself, "Then there is nothing more to think about, is there?"

A Vow to Not Look at Pornography

One day after school, I was standing in the corner drug store when I noticed the first display of a new sensual magazine. Instantly, I recalled with sadness the favorable newspaper articles promoting this new publication. I was grieved as I realized that millions of men and boys would be corrupted in their moral standards by opening its pages and looking at the lewd pictures.

I also remembered the warning of Jesus: "Whosoever looketh on a woman to lust after her hath committed adultery with her already in his heart. [This would also apply to pornography.]

"And if thy right eye offend thee, pluck it out, and cast it from thee: for it is profitable for thee that one of thy members should perish, and not that thy whole body should be cast into hell. And if thy right hand offend thee, cut it off, and cast it from thee: for it is profitable for thee that one of thy members should perish, and not that thy whole body should be cast into hell" (Matthew 5:28–30).

As I stood there, I wondered what I could do to protect people from this and similar magazines. At that moment, the thought came to me: "Suppose that in the future, you were interviewed on a national TV program and asked, 'Have you ever looked inside this magazine?' What would you say?"

I purposed then that I would be able to say "no," and therefore I made a vow that I would never open or look inside this magazine. God has given the grace to keep this vow and extend it to similar magazines.

With the lure of nudity and the invasion of privacy over the Internet, I do not see how it is possible for a young person today to escape the corruption and addiction of pornography without making a firm vow to God to not look at pornography. (See Job 31:1.)

A Vow to Not Watch Sensual TV

While staying in a hotel, I turned on the TV. I was shocked by the immorality that I saw! I wondered why the Federal Communication Commission would allow such a thing to be aired.

I turned the TV off and made a vow that never again would I turn on a TV in a hotel room. That vow was made over thirty-five years ago, and since then I have stayed in hundreds of hotel rooms. Each time, it never even occurs to me to turn on the TV set. To me, it is like a piece of furniture.

One of the many rewards of this vow is having thousands of extra hours to invest in profitable activities that will have eternal value. This vow is among those that I have made to "hate evil." Each vow has been a guiding light on the path of eternal achievement. On the other side, there have been vows that I have made to do things for the Lord and to advance His Kingdom.

Solomon was the wisest man who ever lived, yet in his later years, he gave his heart to immoral women. They drew him away from the Lord, yet he spent the first seven chapters of Proverbs warning young men not to be deceived by women.

"There met him a woman with the attire of a harlot, and subtle of heart. . . . He goeth after her straightway, as an ox goeth to the slaughter, or as a fool to the correction of the stocks; till a dart strike through his liver; as a bird hasteth to the snare, and knoweth not that it is for his life" (Proverbs 7:10, 22–23).

11

The account of John Huss was especially challenging to me. As a boy, he held his finger over a candle flame to see if he was courageous enough to be burned for his faith. Later, he was burned at the stake.

Abraham Lincoln is one of the most revered men in history. More books have been written about his life than about any other President's life. It is interesting to note that he waited for marriage until he reached the age of thirty-three.

A Vow to Die for Jesus

One of the most significant vows I ever made took place when I was about fourteen years old. The details are still vivid in my memory. I was sitting next to a window in my bedroom as I read *Foxe's Book of Martyrs*.

As I read of the torture and temptations that Christians had endured in order to bring the Bible and its message to me, the thought came to my mind, "Would I be willing to die for the Lord?"

After thinking about the implications of doing this, I bowed my head and vowed to the Lord that I would be willing to die for Him and for the advancement of His Kingdom.

A significant result took place. Suddenly, I viewed myself as a runner in a race—a race against time. I wanted to accomplish as much as I could for the Lord before I died. There was no time for frivolous activities or time-consuming sports. I wanted to do things that would count for this life and for the life to come.

This one vow has been a driving motivation and guiding force in my life. It has given meaning and purpose to live for God and a joy in seeing significant things done for Him.

A Vow for Years of Single Ministry

One day when I was about seventeen, my sister Anne came home from high school. My mother and I were standing in the dining room when my sister stated, "I learned something very interesting in school today." My mother asked what it was, and Anne said: "I learned that the average age of marriage for people who accomplish great things and get into *Who's Who in America* is twenty-eight years old. They spend the best years of their youth concentrating on their achievements."

Immediately, I thought to myself, "If they can do it for secular achievements, I can certainly do that for the Lord's work." So right there I vowed that I would wait until I was at least twenty-eight years old before getting married. The race against time now intensified as I worked to accomplish as much as I could before marriage.

In making this vow, I was careful not to vow that I would never marry. I would not encourage anyone to make such a vow. (See I Timothy 4:3.) On the other hand, there are great rewards for those who set aside years for single service. (See Isaiah 56:3–7.)

George Washington, known as the "Father of America," accomplished remarkable achievements before he got married at the age of twenty-seven.

A Vow to Witness to Others

When I was a teenager, a dynamic speaker explained the importance of witnessing to others about the Lord. He then asked all of us to make a vow to talk to an average of three people each day about Christ.

I raised my hand and made that vow. During high school I was able to keep it, because every year I tried to share the Gospel with all of my classmates. However, after high school my schedule changed, and I did not keep this vow.

Years later, through a series of circumstances, God reminded me of that vow, and I purposed to "catch up." I got into my car, drove to Chicago, and began looking for street gangs.

For eight months, I met with groups of young people in various parts of the city and suburbs of Chicago. What I learned during those months became an important part of the teaching that I later gave in the Basic Youth Conflicts Seminar.

Each time I met a new street gang, I asked them if they would like me to give them a scenic "chalk-talk" that answered life's three big questions: Where did I come from? Why am I here? and Where will I go after death? All answered, "Yes!" What I learned gave me the foundation for effective youth work.

13

The Foundation of the Basic Seminar

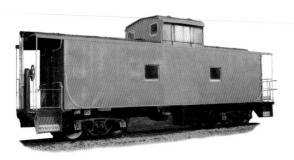

For nine summers during high school, college, and graduate school, I worked for the Burlington Northern Railroad.

Each morning I would take the train to the last stop before Chicago, walk over to a caboose, and change into my work clothes in preparation for the jobs of the day.

Spending those evenings on a railroad car and memorizing the Sermon on the Mount gave the structure I later used to teach the Basic Youth Conflicts Seminar. This was one of the richest experiences of my life, because it opened up my understanding of the importance of the commands of Christ.

My job for the first summer was as a painter's helper for paint gang number three. Three older men were on that team.

One morning I noticed that there was a vacant bedroom on one side of the caboose. That gave me an idea. I asked the supervisor if I could stay overnight in that room for several weeks so that I could carry out a special project. He asked what the project was, and I said, "I want to memorize the Sermon on the Mount." He looked surprised but said, "Yes, you can."

Each morning I stood on the platform of the Stone Avenue Station in LaGrange Illinois (pictured above), waiting for the train to take me into work, until that special day when I decided to stay on the caboose in order to have quietness and more time to memorize Scripture.

I still remember the shock I had when I walked into the room that first night and saw inappropriate pictures on the wall. I quickly took them down and put them out of sight. It never entered my mind to look at them during those weeks in which I was memorizing the powerful truths of Matthew 5, 6, and 7.

Each day as I painted train signals over the tracks or a railroad station, I would meditate on the verses that I had memorized the previous night. Those chapters made up the belief system of my heart and were engrafted into my mind, will, and emotions. From them God has opened up great treasures of truth that have enriched my life in ways I never thought possible.

The Writing of the Textbook

As I approached my thirtieth birthday, an exciting idea came to me: "When Jesus was thirty, he spent forty days in the wilderness fasting and praying. Why couldn't I do the same?"

I received permission to use a vacant lodge in the Northwoods camp owned by Wheaton College. On the first day of January, I climbed into my 1957 Ford convertible and began the journey. The temperature was 30 below 0, and the wind whipped through the roof that covered the convertible.

When I arrived at Camp Honey Rock, about three feet of snow was covering the ground. Paul, the caretaker, showed me to my room. The next forty days were the turning point of my life!

During those marvelous days of seeking the Lord and the treasures of His Word, I alternated between reading large portions of Scripture, memorizing and meditating on key verses, reading the biographies of great Christians and other classic Christian books, singing hymns, and writing down the principles of youth work that I had learned during the past fifteen years.

For the first twenty days, the room temperature was 60 degrees. (My comfort range is between 75 and 85 degrees.) Then I discovered a thermostat on the wall and turned the heat up. The temperature was not that important, however, as I experienced fellowship with God in ways that I never had experienced before.

By the end of the forty days, I had finished the textbook on youth work. It was based on the Beatitudes of the Sermon on the Mount.

Shortly thereafter I was invited to speak for a week of meetings at Kansas City Bible College. As I shared with them the commands of Christ and their practical

God rewarded that first January in the Northwoods in such a marvelous way that I determined to repeat it for as many years as I could. I have now spent forty-six Januarys in the Northwoods. Each one has been an exciting adventure into God's truth and way of life. The Chalet at Camp Honey Rock (pictured above) was the location of my first extended fast.

The Northwoods Conference Center has become the location of my annual time with God. The rewards of giving God the first month of the year have proven to be a remarkable way of being blessed by Him.

The Basic Seminar taught Christ's commands:

1. Love your neighbor as yourself. (See Matthew 22:39.) Loving others requires that we accept the way God *designed* us.

2. Honor your father and mother. (See Matthew 15:4.) Honoring *authority* must be distinguished from blind obedience.

3. Be reconciled. (See Matthew 5:24–25.) Gaining a *clear conscience* with those we have offended.

4. Forgive offenders. (See Matthew 18:21–22.) Avoiding bitterness with full *forgiveness*.

5. Take my yoke. (See Matthew 11:29.) *Yielding rights* conquers anger.

6. Do not lust. (See Matthew 5:29.) Allowing the Spirit to control physical drives brings moral *freedom*.

7. Keep Christ's commands. (See John 14:15.) Meditation on Scripture brings *success*.

applications, a revival broke out among the student body. I was up until 2 and 3 in the morning, counseling students who were thrilled to get practical answers for their lives.

The president exclaimed: "In all my years, I have never witnessed a response like this. This is a true revival!" He then asked me to return the following year, which I did.

The Basic Seminar Is Launched

After returning from Kansas City, I was invited by Wheaton College to teach a summer course on what I had learned in my fifteen years of youth work. Wheaton named the course "Basic Youth Conflicts."

The first course was offered in 1964, and 46 students enrolled. This included youth pastors, college students, and some of my graduate school professors. The second year, 120 students enrolled. Many came from other cities because of the reports of those who had attended the first year.

The third year, a total of 1,000 attended three seminars held at Trinity College in Deerfield, Illinois. The ones who attended these seminars were not just taking a course; as they applied the truths they were learning from the commands of Christ, their lives were being transformed! They kept telling their friends about what they had learned, and by 1972 more than 128,000 had registered for what had been developed into a thirty-hour seminar, the Basic Youth Conflicts Seminar.

The next year, 200,000 attended, and then there were 350,000 the following year! All these registrations were the result of enthusiastic word-of-mouth recommendations. There was no media advertising. To date, more than 2.7 million youth and adults have attended a Basic Seminar. Many have returned to repeat the course, bringing the total attendance to more than 7 million!

Year after year, "The Omni" in Atlanta, Georgia, was packed with youth and adults.

In Dallas, Texas, this arena was filled, with an overflow crowd of ten thousand people.

Cobo Hall in Detroit was one of sixteen coliseums across America that were filled each year.

The Seminar in California filled the Long Beach Arena, with an overflow of five thousand.

After pastors from Minneapolis attended a Seminar, they asked for one in their city. They rented an auditorium for 800, but 8,000 people registered to attend the Seminar. Six months later, 16,000 attended. The third Seminar attracted 27,500.

As I would look out over an audience of thousands of eager and attentive youth and adults, I would often ask myself: "What is drawing these people here? It cannot be me, because I am not an eloquent speaker."

Then, one Christmas when I was in Russia, our director there, Bob Bair, said to me, "Bill, have you ever counted the number of Christ's commands that you actually teach in the Basic Seminar?"

The Lord promises great rewards for keeping all of His commands in our heart and mind. Through them, He has promised to reveal Himself to us: "He that hath my commandments, and keepeth them, he it is that loveth me: and he that loveth me shall be loved of my Father, and I will love him, and will manifest myself to him" (John 14:21).

That night I took the list of forty-nine general commands of Christ that I had found in the Gospels and matched them with the content in the Basic Seminar.

Herbert J. Taylor was an amazingly successful businessman in Chicago. He bought a bankrupt company for $6,000 and turned it into a multimillion-dollar corporation. When I asked him what his secret was, he said, "Throughout every day, I quote the Sermon on the Mount."

Further Rewards for Keeping Christ's Commands

1. We will be His friend: "Ye are my friends, if ye do whatsoever I command you" (John 15:14).

2. Our prayers will be answered: "Whatsoever we ask, we receive of him, because we keep his commandments . . ." (I John 3:22).

3. We will abide in His love: "If ye keep my commandments, ye shall abide in my love" (John 15:10).

4. We will love others: "By this we know that we love the children of God, when we love God, and keep his commandments" (I John 5:2).

5. We will know God: "And hereby we do know that we know him, if we keep his commandments" (I John 2:3).

6. God will live in us: "If a man love me, he will keep my words: and my Father will love him, and we will come unto him, and make our abode with him" (John 14:23).

To my amazement, I discovered how all forty-nine commands are either explained, illustrated, or referred to in the Seminar! No wonder there is power that transforms lives, marriages, families, businesses, and churches when these are applied.

A "New" Approach to Education!

When parents saw the transforming power of teaching Christ's commands, they asked if we could develop a curriculum so that they could home-educate their sons and daughters using the principles they had learned in the Basic Seminar.

We took the fifty-four concepts in the Sermon on the Mount and developed a booklet on each one. They ranged anywhere from sixteen to eighty-four pages. Other academic subjects were built around each topic.

For example, Jesus said, "Ye are the salt of the earth" (Matthew 5:13). Therefore, we studied the etymology of words in our vocabulary about salt (such as *salary*— payments of salt), where salt is located and how it is mined, the history of salt and its uses, the science of salt and how its crystals are formed, the medical aspects of salt and how it is essential for the functioning of the body, and the legal aspects of salt (salt treaties and salt covenants). The finished project turned out to be five thousand pages of information and instruction, including a parent guide on how to teach the material.

In 1984, the Advanced Training Institute was launched, and by 1990 we had a host of students that were so outstanding that they captured the attention of nations around the world.

Fifteen thousand ATI parents and students gathered at Knoxville University.

New Zealand

The Prime Minister of New Zealand invited our ministry to come to his nation and help them celebrate "the year of New Zealand."

When we arrived, a U.S. Embassy official asked me what we were going to do in the country. I replied that we were going to conduct a Basic Youth Conflicts Seminar. He laughed and declared, "This is the most secular nation in the world!" Then he casually asked, "How many people do you think will attend your Seminar?"

He expected me to say 20 or 30, which was a normal size for such an event. When I mentioned that more than 3,000 had already registered, his mouth fell open, he lurched forward, and he repeated with disbelief, "Three thousand?!" I replied, "Yes, and there are another 2,500 registered for Christchurch in the South Island and 1,500 in the capital city of Wellington."

Pictured above is New Zealand's Capitol, "The Beehive."
A delegation from New Zealand arrived in 1989 with a letter of invitation from the Prime Minister and most of the major Christian leaders of that nation.

Pictured above is the original team of staff members and students who traveled to Russia and met with school officials in Moscow. The officials were so impressed with these young people that they asked if the group could return in the fall to host a Basic Seminar.

The returning group is pictured below. We chartered a Russian airliner for the trip.

Russia

The next year I heard that Bibles were being given out in Russian public schools! I thought: "That is amazing! How could we encourage them?"

A few days later, a director of a Christian organization from Florida visited our Headquarters. He was looking for outstanding examples of Christian young people who could go to Russia and pass out Scripture portions.

When the director met the student staff, he exclaimed, "You are the perfect ones to go!" We selected forty-six young people, along with Dr. Roy Blackwood and his wife, Margie, for the trip.

When we arrived in Moscow, we met Dr. Mitskovky, who worked with the public schools of Moscow. I was talking with him as our students filed in behind me. When he saw our young people, he said to me, "Please excuse me; I must make a phone call!"

He rushed into a side room and called Galena, the Director of Moscow Orphanages, and said, "You must come over here and see these young people!" She replied, "I am busy with appointments all morning."

He said: "No, you must come over here. You have never seen a group like this before!"

When Galena arrived and saw our group, she was

stunned! At a later ATI Conference of 15,000 family members, she recalled, "When I saw your young people, I concluded that they were somewhere between human beings and angels!"

She invited us to return in the fall to present a Basic Seminar in Moscow and to work in the public schools. That fall we chartered a Russian airliner and filled it with three hundred young people, our Board of Directors, and special guests.

This was the first Aeroflot Russian airliner ever to land at Chicago's O'Hare Airport. The flight was arranged by the Russian government to fly our team over to work with their students, orphans, and pensioner teachers.

When we arrived in Moscow, we went to the Department of Education headquarters and filled

When the Mayor and city officials in Moscow saw the valuable service we gave, they provided a five-acre campus with three multi-story buildings free of charge for seventeen years.

This flight launched regular air service between Moscow and Chicago.

The Deputy Mayor of Moscow met with us to explain the needs of the city and then presented us with a pictorial book of Moscow.

President Boris Yeltsin and his wife were so impressed with our ATI students that they sent their grandson back to America with them.

23

Each year for seventeen years, the Moscow Department of Education bused in 2,500 of their neediest pensioner teachers for a banquet and a special program, including a chalk-talk and a gift equal to a month's salary.

A deep bond was established between our students and the pensioner teachers.

their auditorium. This had been the former Moscow Communist Party headquarters.

Galena went up to the fifth floor to invite the head of the Department of Education of Moscow, Dr. Kezina, to meet us. She replied very firmly, "No, I am busy with appointments!"

Galena replied: "You must come and see this group! They are the most outstanding students I have ever met, and they are from America." Dr. Kezina stated, "I have been to America, and I have seen their young people, and I am not impressed!" The final plea was, "But these are Christian young people!" Dr. Kezina answered, "I have also been to Christian schools in America, and I am not impressed with them either!"

Dr. Kezina finally consented to come down to the auditorium and just peek into the room. When she looked at the three hundred radiant ATI students, she said, "Cancel all my appointments!" Then she walked up to the podium, took the microphone, and stated, "What I see here is what I want all my students to be like, and I will do whatever I can to make that happen!"

Dr. Kezina kept her word. On our return trip, we brought over five hundred young people and rented two ships in the Moscow River to house them. That was our base to teach in their public schools, work with orphanages, visit youth prisons, and sponsor annual banquets for thousands of needy pensioner teachers.

At a large gathering of teachers, I was sitting next to Dr. Kezina, listening to

These banquets were the annual highlight for the needy pensioners and for us as well.

a choir of several hundred. Among the group were Russian students, along with our young people.

Dr. Kezina turned to me and with excitement stated: "Look at that group! They are outstanding, and I cannot tell which ones are Russians and which ones are Americans!"

Two Basic Seminars were held in the two major Moscow sports arenas, with a total of more than eight thousand attending. During the Basic Seminar, our students conducted a children's program for hundreds of Russian children whose parents were at the Basic Seminar. This was so successful that the education students from the University of Moscow rushed over to see how we could train hundreds of active Russian children to be so attentive that they literally could hear a pin drop!

The Mayor of Moscow and all ten Moscow school districts presented us with prestigious awards and certificates of gratefulness after ten years of serving in their city and public schools.

The Republic of China—Taiwan

When the education officials in Taiwan heard about the work that we were doing in Russian schools, they invited us to visit their nation.

We arrived with about 170 of our young people. I still remember sitting next to the Minister of Education of Taipei as he watched our students sing. He turned to me and exclaimed, "If I had students like this in my school, we would never have any problems!"

A Basic Seminar was held, with three thousand attending. Then, the Minister of Education

After arriving in Taiwan, we were taken to the presidential palace to have a special meeting with President Lee and his chief assistant. During our meeting, superintendents of Russian public schools told the President of our work in their schools and urged Taiwan to follow their example.

Six thousand of Taiwan's public school students, mostly Buddhists, stood at attention as our students told them how the principles of God's way of life had impacted their lives. Soon it began to rain, and the Taiwanese students told their instructors that they wanted to stay out in the rain so that they would not miss anything that we were telling them.

asked if we could send our students to teach in their public schools. We have been doing this for the past nineteen years!

After the first year, a team of twelve TV, newspaper, and magazine reporters representing eight media outlets came to our training centers to see how we were training our students. Then they aired a series of nationally broadcasted TV programs on prime time, stating, "If you want a new way of education, then learn about this program."

At one point, the Minister of Education in Taiwan asked all of our teachers to visit him in his office. The first question he asked was, "Why do our Taiwanese schoolchildren love you so much?" Our students answered: "We believe that there are three reasons: First, because they know that we love them. Second, because we teach them character qualities. Third, because we keep their attention through creativity in teaching."

Top education officials in Kaohsiung City listened during a five-day Seminar as universal Biblical principles were explained to them. This event was sponsored by the Taiwanese government and repeated in two other cities.

Today, any of our students who want to teach in the public schools of Taiwan will be flown there free of charge and given free room, board, and a monthly financial stipend of $800, plus special vacations—all without a college diploma. One district has offered to pay a year of college expenses at our Verity Institute for every extra year of service we give them!

Romania

Mayors from Romania attended a mayors' conference that was held in 1996. When they met our students, they invited us to come to Romania.

During our annual mayors' conferences, delegations from Romania attended and urged us to sign agreements of cooperation with them.

When we arrived in their nation, we had several meetings with high-level officials. At each meeting, they urged us to sign an agreement of cooperation in which our students would work in their schools, as well as in other capacities. We have had the privilege of doing this for the past fourteen years!

In recent years, we have had the honor of bringing approximately four hundred Romanian officials to our Headquarters for a week of training. Mayors, education officials, police officers, judges, governors, medical officials, and religious leaders have been among these guests. We are now in the process of expanding our work in Romania.

The Romanian delegation pictured above had us sign an agreement with the Ministry of the Interior to provide training to their 100,000 employees.

Teachers in Romania are granted fifteen hours of continuing education credit if they complete our character training course and teach character to their students.

The Minister of Education signs a historic agreement for the Institute to teach character and Biblical principles to the 4 million schoolchildren and 100,000 orphans in Romania. This agreement provides the basis of our present teaching in Romanian schools.

In order to serve the city of Indianapolis, we were able to purchase a vacant hotel and remodel it in order to accommodate thousands of students who came for special training and service.

Indianapolis

When Mayor Stephen Goldsmith heard about our work in Moscow, he invited us to Indianapolis. Our first assignment was to send hundreds of students into high-crime areas for neighborhood cleanup. Then the juvenile court system turned over to us its most difficult delinquents to see what would happen. The results were so significant that court systems in other states also sent us their repeat offenders.

The DuPage County Juvenile Court System in Illinois sent us a sixteen-year-old girl who had been arrested more than seventy times on various charges. Six months later, as a result of the dramatic changes in her life, *The Indianapolis Star* featured a full-page story about this young woman.

The log cabin concept of working with troubled youth was established at the Indianapolis Training Center, where the first cabin was built. This program involved two mature young men mentoring a troubled young person on a day-to-day basis.

Then they asked if we would take a fifteen-year-old boy named Kevin. His one goal in life was to destroy America and kill as many people as he could in the process. At every court appearance, deputies lined the pathways so that Kevin would not destroy things. After we agreed to work with him, the juvenile detention center called us up and begged us to take him immediately, because he was destroying their facility.

Three months later, Kevin was teaching character qualities to public school students in Indianapolis, alongside our students. After he finished his training, Kevin asked if he could continue on by serving at the training center, which he did.

Little Rock

News of our work in Indianapolis reached the Mayor of Little Rock, Arkansas, Jim Dailey. He flew up to our training center and went out with one of the cleanup teams that was working in Fountain Square. What he saw so impressed him that he asked if we would come to Little Rock and serve his city.

Mayor Dailey invited us to come to Little Rock, and we asked him whether he would like us to carry out a little program or a big program for the city. He said, "A big program." Based on that, we secured a 500,000-square-foot former VA hospital.

Through the generosity of Hobby Lobby, we were provided with a 500,000-square-foot former veterans' hospital for our use. One area of the building was then remodeled and leased to the city without charge, to house the district police station of about 170 policemen.

At about the same time, a prison ministry was launched from this facility under the direction of Chaplain Bob Holyfield. He began working with prison officials throughout America to show the Basic Seminar and give character training to the prisoners. The transformations in their lives and the dramatic decrease of conflicts in the prisons motivated other prisons to request the program. Currently we are serving in 150 prisons. The recidivism rate has been drastically reduced in each of these prisons. One prisoner even asked if he could stay in prison so that he could complete the training.

When Mayor Dailey went out with hundreds of our students to a high-crime neighborhood in Indianapolis and watched them serve the city with joy and excitement, he concluded, "These are the kinds of young people I want in my city."

The Expanding Outreach

The universal nature of the Basic Seminar and the message it teaches continue to open doors in cities, states, and nations around the world. All of these works are powerful testimonies of what can happen when we learn and apply the commands of Christ.

Fifty students and staff members traveled by bus to Mexico.

After we spoke in this village, the Mayor asked if we could return the next week.

Mexico

When I visited two orphanages in Monterrey, Mexico, I offered to train twenty of their most promising orphans how to be character coaches so that they could return in six months and teach their fellow students. The one who was designated to select the orphans misinterpreted the instructions and sent us their twenty worst-behaving orphans. They were a challenge! After three months, government officials visited and exclaimed, "You have done more in three months than we have been able to do in many years!"

When our time of speaking to hundreds of students was over, the Mayor's wife asked if we could extend our visit. From there, we went to a large orphanage in Guadalajara and spoke to two thousand boys who listened attentively for four hours as we explained how Christ's commands had transformed our lives.

ATI student Erik Phariss, pictured with President Fox

The Philippines

When Mayor Talentino of Tagaytay City attended a mayors' conference at our Indianapolis Training Center, he was extremely impressed with our ATI students and with

When the teenage orphans arrived at our Headquarters, we challenged them to become international character coaches.

the character training that they had received. When he returned to the Philippines, he and his staff passed a resolution to make his city a City of Character.

They built a multimillion-dollar convention center and gave each room a character name. The streets of the city also were given character names, and before couples could receive their marriage licenses, they were required to pass a course on character training. This city is now a model for other cities, and its success is recognized throughout the Philippines.

Secretary Cabral, who coordinated this trip, answers directly to the President of the Philippines. She was so encouraged with the results of our training that she asked us to expand our work. She is responsible for 27 million needy people.

In 2004, the Secretary of the Department of Social Welfare and Development asked us to train twenty-four teenage orphans. After six months, they returned to the Philippines and have continued to teach in orphanages, parks, and at city events.

Most of these boys grew up on the streets of Manila and had extremely painful memories from their childhoods. The love and acceptance that they received from our staff and students met a deep need in their lives. The young man pictured above sobbed with gratefulness as he gave me a strong embrace. His mother tried to sell him when he was a boy, and he became an abandoned child who lived on the streets.

31

WEALTH

. . . is not in our hands to get or keep but in God's hands to give and receive.

2

The Way to
LASTING WEALTH:

Become a Generous Giver!

It was not easy for me to learn to be generous! At a very young age, I was a confirmed "penny pincher." Every dollar I earned went into my savings account at the First National Bank of LaGrange.

By the time I entered high school, I was very proud of all the money I had earned. I actually felt sympathy for fellow students who were not as financially well off as I thought I was.

As a young boy, I opened a savings account at this bank and viewed it as my way to success. But God had important lessons for me to learn about money.

I never will forget that Sunday morning when God "invaded" my financial world. I was listening to a representative of The Gideons International as he explained how they provide New Testaments for schoolchildren. God then reminded me of a passage in the Bible: "Lay not up for yourselves treasures upon earth, where moth and rust doth corrupt, and where thieves break through and steal: but lay up for yourselves treasures in heaven, where neither moth nor rust doth corrupt, and where thieves do not break through

On Sunday morning at this church, God talked to me about my bank account and changed the course of my life.

33

This was The Gideons International headquarters when my father was the executive director. During his tenure, he received a telegram from General Douglas MacArthur requesting millions of New Testaments and a thousand missionaries for Japan.

As my father read the telegram from General MacArthur, I saw the pain in his face. He could send the New Testaments, but he had no missionaries to send. This motivated me to train young people who could travel quickly to a nation when an opportunity opened up.

nor steal. For where your treasure is, there will your heart be also" (Matthew 6:19–21).

I realized that my treasure and my heart were securely stored in the First National Bank of LaGrange. I knew what God had in mind for my hard-earned bank account. At twenty cents a Testament, I figured out how many I could sponsor with all of my money. The struggle between doing what I knew God wanted and hanging on to what I desired became intense!

Then the second Biblical "bomb" dropped from heaven—another passage that I had memorized: "Will a man rob God? Yet ye have robbed me. But ye say, Wherein have we robbed thee? In tithes and offerings" (Malachi 3:8). That was convicting! I suddenly realized that I had never given God His portion of any of the dollars I had earned.

Negotiating With God

I began to negotiate with God: "Lord, I will give you 10% of my bank account!" Somehow, that idea did not seem to even reach the ceiling. So, I upped the offer: "I will give you 50% of all that I have earned."

It was then that the rest of the passage came to my mind: "Prove me now herewith, saith the LORD of hosts, if I will not open you the windows of heaven, and pour you out a blessing, that there shall not be room enough to receive it" (Malachi 3:10). That settled the matter. I wanted to prove God with 100% of my money. This meant taking the funds that I was going to use to buy a car and turning them into New Testaments for schoolchildren.

What happened during the following year is an amazing testimony of God's ability to open up the windows of heaven and shower out blessings. It is important to note that the passage does not say "shower out money," because the blessings of God usually involve things that are more valuable than money, such as faith, fellowship with God, inward peace, joy, genuine love, health, and creativity.

Not only did God give me back twice the money I had given Him, but He also gave me a car better than I could have purchased with the money I had given away.

God's "Windows" Open Up

God did choose to confirm that He also could pour out money for the things that I needed. A man who worked for a steel company learned that I had built a photo lab in my basement. He asked if I would be able to develop film of highly magnified steel. The molecular structure of the steel would reveal the various types of alloys and their relative strengths. I gladly did the work after school, and he paid me very well for it.

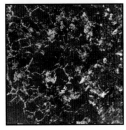

By the next year, in the bank I had twice the amount of money that I had given away, plus a car that was better than one I could have purchased with all of those resources! This amazed me!

I was thrilled with my car and my increased bank account. God saw my excitement and discerned that my excitement for money and possessions was stronger than my delight in Him, the Giver of all good things. He knew that I still needed some further lessons on

The metallography that I was asked to do revealed the alloys of steel to determine its relative strength and durability. My work for this steel company was later used as an entry for a Future Scientists and Engineers of America contest, which won a top award.

35

There was no reason for my car to stop on the highway since I had just gotten it fixed. There was also no reason why the vehicle behind me did not see that I had stopped. Its headlights became larger and brighter as I realized that God was getting ready to take me through a new experience.

When we give something to God, it instantly becomes holy because it belongs to Him. He is then free to take it from us or to allow us to continue using it. In either case, we must be prepared to thank Him for whatever He chooses to do.

how to conquer my focus on money and look to Him as the source for all my needs. Therefore, He arranged for the following event to take place.

The Lord Gives and Takes Away

One evening as I was driving home after a meeting, my car suddenly stalled. I thought, "This is strange; I just spent money to get it all tuned up." I looked in the rearview mirror and saw the headlights of an approaching vehicle. The lights were getting larger and larger very quickly, coming up right behind me. I wondered if the driver saw me, so I blinked my taillights several times. His headlights were still in my lane and getting very big and very bright.

I realized that he was going to hit my car. Therefore, I slid down in the driver's seat so that my head would not get jerked back, and I held onto the steering wheel, waiting for the impact that would catapult me down the road.

A moment later I felt and heard a terrific crash. My car went skidding down the highway! I was uninjured, so I climbed out of the car to survey the new "accordion design" of my car!

A New Perspective on the Crash

After getting the necessary information from the driver who had hit me, I realized that I was not going anywhere with that car, so I ran down the road to look for a phone to call a tow truck. As I ran, I experienced a spirit of joy and excitement!

When I tell this to people, they often give me a funny look, and I know what they are thinking: "Bill, why were you so happy? Are you sure nothing happened to *you* in that accident?"

I was joyful because I was able to say to God: "Lord, I dedicated that car to You. It's Your car. If You want to wreck Your car, that is all right with me!"

For several months, I was without a car, because I had no money; I also had given away that *second* bank account. God had me in just the right position for Him to demonstrate this promise: "Give, and it shall be given unto you; good measure, pressed down, and shaken together, and running over, shall men give into your bosom" (Luke 6:38).

One day a man called up and said: "Bill, I have a nine-passenger station wagon. I would like to give it to you for your youth work." I thanked him and picked up the car.

Several days later, another man called and said: "Bill, I have a car I am not using any more. Could you use it?" I never like to turn things down, so I got it too. Then Chuck Sebastian, the owner of one of the radio stations over which I was broadcasting my Saturday morning radio programs, called and said: "Bill, I want to give you a car. It is very fast." It certainly was! It was a "souped-up" Simca and went 60 miles an hour in second gear—with the brakes on!

The cars pictured above represent the styles of the cars, but not the actual cars, given to me.

The following event took place in Bartlett Hall (pictured above), which was my dorm at Wheaton College.

I lived in that dorm for an entire year. Only once do I remember that phone ever ringing, and it was just at the moment of need with just the message I needed to hear. God is precise with His timing and His provisions.

Notice God's sequence: "Give, and it shall be given unto you" (Luke 6:38). In other words, we must initiate the giving.

Then, a medical doctor called to say that he was giving me his air-conditioned Lincoln car! Before long I was sitting at my desk, flipping through car titles. There were seven of them—more than my driveway could handle! God surely did open up the windows of heaven and pour out a blessing beyond what I had imagined!

A "Hug" From My Loving God

After attending junior college for two years, I went on to Wheaton College for the remaining two years. One beautiful warm spring afternoon, I was walking to my dorm when I realized that it was my mother's birthday and I would be going home that evening. I said, "Lord, You have all my money, and it would be nice if I had twenty dollars to buy a gift for my mother."

Just as I entered my dorm, the phone in the hallway rang. No one else was there, so I picked it up. I heard a man's voice say, "Is there someone there who would like to earn a little money?" I said: "Yes! Me!" He said: "I need someone to dig a trench in my backyard. It should only take about an hour." I told him that I would love to do it!

It was delightful to be outdoors and get some exercise by digging that trench. As he drove me back to my dorm, he explained that he was a descendant of P. T. Barnum of circus fame. As I got out of the car, he handed me something—a twenty-dollar bill! I thanked him for his generosity and then just looked at that bill. That was not just a coincidence. It had been arranged by God to show His attention to the details of my needs. It was like a great big hug from God, Who "loveth a cheerful giver" (II Corinthians 9:7).

A Mansion and a Miracle

There is a historic mansion on Lake Geneva. It was built at the turn of the century by Otto Young, a wealthy businessman in Chicago. It had a breathtaking interior, including huge marble fireplaces, domed ceilings with Rembrandt-type paintings on them, and a marble-columned ballroom.

The inlaid floors and the intricately carved ceiling molding were awesome! There was a magnificent, wide, winding, mahogany staircase to the second and third floors. In each bedroom was a hand-carved marble fireplace (imported from Italy), and a stunning, unique pattern of inlaid wood embellished the floor of each room. I asked the owner if we could use the mansion for a weekend retreat, and he allowed us to do so. The building could hold up to 150 teenagers.

When the young people walked into the building, their mouths dropped open in awe as they looked at the splendor of the interior. The surroundings motivated them to be attentive during each session. The retreat was so successful that I asked if we could hold a series of meetings there. The owner agreed.

A view of the fifty-room mansion on Lake Geneva

Some of the ornate detail in the grand ballroom, which was carried throughout the building and even in the kitchen, where sculptured wood molding was used in the ceilings. Beautiful murals were painted in the domes of the ceilings between the marble columns.

Early in my high school years, I often would go to a forest preserve south of my home early in the morning to seek the Lord. It was a special secluded area off the beaten path that became my "Bethel." A large fallen log served as both my bench from which to read the Scriptures and also my altar from which to pray. Precious times were experienced with the Lord during these early morning watches.

"My voice shalt thou hear in the morning, O Lord; in the morning will I direct my prayer unto thee, and will look up" (Psalm 5:3).

An "Insurmountable" Challenge Faced Us

On the Sunday before the first retreat was to begin, the owner said, "Bill, you cannot come up here with your retreats!" I was stunned and asked, "Why not?" He said: "Because the fire marshal came out and said that we must install a fire alarm system in the building. If we do not have it installed, he will padlock the building."

I thought of all the work and money that had gone into the planning of those retreats and the hundreds of young people who were already registered to come. So I asked, "How long would it take to get the fire alarm system installed?"

He explained the procedure: "First, the plans must be drawn up and submitted to the city. After they are approved, you must order the fire alarm equipment from the factory. After they make it and ship it out, it must be installed and inspected. There is no human way to get all of that done in five days!" I asked, "If we do get it in, will you let us go ahead with the retreats?" He laughed and said, "Sure!"

Immediately, I called my friend Charlie Reavis, who was an electrician. I said, "Charlie, I have a special need that I am hoping you can take care of." He asked what it was, and I replied, "We need to install an alarm system in the mansion at Lake Geneva." He asked, "When does it need to be in?" I said, "By this Friday!" He gasped and said: "That would be humanly impossible! I have rush orders at the factory now from customers who have been waiting for several weeks!" I said, "What if we just try and see what happens?" He agreed.

On Friday, I drove up to Lake Geneva. As I pulled into the drive, another car pulled in behind me. It was the city fire inspector. We walked into the building together and saw Charlie on a ladder, putting the final adjustments on the alarm system. He called out to his assistant, "Try it out again!" We heard the resounding alarm throughout the building! What a beautiful sound!

Several months later Charlie gave a testimony at a youth rally about what actually had happened during those five days. He broke down in tears as he explained how God had worked supernaturally on his behalf, through split-second timing and the favor of all who had been involved. In more than thirty years of electrical work, he had never before experienced anything like it. He said that he would never forget being involved in a true miracle, and many of those hundreds of young people who attended the retreats never forgot the spiritual decisions they made because of his work.

The goal of our life should not be to acquire things but to look for opportunities in which God can demonstrate His love and power: "The eyes of the LORD run to and fro throughout the whole earth, to show himself strong in the behalf of them whose heart is perfect toward him" (II Chronicles 16:9).

An Amazing Opportunity

Several years later, the owner of the Lake Geneva mansion came to see me and said, "The mansion is being sold for back taxes!" I asked him how much was owed on the taxes, and he said, "Seventy-four thousand dollars!"

I asked in astonishment, "Are you telling me that someone could buy that mansion for only $74,000?!" He said: "Yes, and I own the first mortgage and would

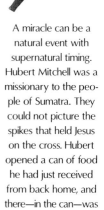

A miracle can be a natural event with supernatural timing. Hubert Mitchell was a missionary to the people of Sumatra. They could not picture the spikes that held Jesus on the cross. Hubert opened a can of food he had just received from back home, and there—in the can—was a large spike!

41

God has performed many miracles through history. In a technical sense, a miracle is a natural or supernatural event with precise timing that brings glory to God.

Dr. Kenneth Taylor, author of *The Living Bible,* was led by the Lord to call on just the right day and offer just the right amount. Dr. Taylor originally wrote the paraphrase that was used for *The Living Bible* while he was riding the train to work each morning. His goal was to read it to his children and help them get a better understanding of the Bible. More than 40 million copies have been sold.

be willing to sell it to you for $10,000. If you own this, you could pay the taxes and get the building."

It sounded too good to be true! I was aware of the great potential that the building had, and I would be thrilled if the Lord provided it for us. The owner stated: "I need to go on a trip, but I will return in two days. If you have the money, I will sell you the first mortgage. If you do not have the money, I have another person who wants to buy it."

After he left, I had a little talk with God: "Lord, You have directed us not to ask people for money. However, there is a businessman I know who might like to give us the money that we need for this mortgage."

Immediately, I sensed the Lord saying, "Bill, if I want you to have this, I can provide it without any help from you!"

The next morning, I woke up with special anticipation: "What is God going to do today about this opportunity?" I went to the office and had no sooner sat down at my desk than the phone rang. I was so excited that I picked it up before anyone else could get to it.

I heard the voice of a man whom I was certainly not expecting to call. He said, "Bill, what is new in your work?" I had a strong urge to say, "We need $10,000 today!" but I sensed God saying: "Bill, keep your hands off of this. If I want to show My power, I can do it without any help from you!"

So I simply said, "Why do you ask?" He replied, "God has directed me to give you $10,000 today— that is, if you can use it!" I was amazed and excited! I explained, "If you would have called yesterday, there would have been no need for it, and if you would have called tomorrow, it would have been too late!"

The man who called was the author of *The Living Bible*—Dr. Ken Taylor. He was a dear friend who is now with the Lord and enjoying his rewards. God demonstrated His power, even though further factors influenced us not to acquire the mansion.

A Boost From a Bump

It was truly a joy to bring a bill before the Lord and ask Him for His direction in paying it. Sometimes He would provide a job; other times, He would have someone give me a gift that was just the right amount, and sometimes He would use unexpected means.

One day I received a bill for my car insurance. It was for $168. I had just given my bank account to God, and so I asked Him for direction in paying this bill. That very day, I had to run an errand to a nearby town. As I approached the ramp leading onto Route 83 and Ogden Avenue, I waited for some cars to pass. Suddenly I felt a slight bump on my back bumper. A large truck had been behind me, and he had not noticed that I was stopped in front of him.

We both looked at the little dent in my bumper, and I said: "It is so little. Don't worry about it!" He said: "No, no. This is why we carry insurance. We will take care of it."

A few days later, his insurance adjuster came to my home to look at the car. I told him that it was really a small dent and that I probably would not get it repaired. He said: "You can do whatever you want with the money. My job is to settle this claim by giving you the money for the bumper." He looked in his price book, and he wrote out a check. He handed it to me, and I just stared at the amount—$168!

George Müller was a man of great faith and a great inspiration to me. He trusted God alone for the care of thousands of orphans in England. However, his purpose was not just to provide for orphans but also to demonstrate to the Christians of his day that they did not need to hoard their money, because God was able to provide what they needed if they first gave their riches to Him.

One time, the cupboards at the orphanage were bare, but the children thanked God for their daily bread. Just then, a knock came at the door. There stood a delivery man whose truck had broken down nearby. Since he could not deliver his truckload of bread to market, he had come to ask if they could use any bread. He gave them his truckload of bread—God's provision!

43

This is the house in LaGrange Park that we purchased with God's confirmation of $94. Plans to construct on addition in the back proceeded after God confirmed that direction with an initial gift of $500.

Several young couples from this church attended a Basic Seminar and began sending gifts for the ministry. One gift arrived on just the right day with the exact amount needed.

The $94 Confirmation

As the need for more staff increased, we looked for a house for a family whom we had invited to serve with us—Larry and Mildred Goring and their children. Larry had been my cook at summer camps and was the best cook I had ever met. Mildred was a Godly woman who knew how to pray.

I heard about a house offered at a good price, so we made up a contract and put a thousand dollars down on it. Our bookkeeper informed me that we were $94 short in our building fund to cover that check. So I said to Karen, a new secretary, "I would not be surprised if God sent in $94 today!" She looked puzzled and said: "Why $94? Why not $95 or $100?" I replied, "God usually confirms our financial decisions by sending in the exact amount!"

The mail arrived. There were eight letters. Karen eagerly said, "Let's open the mail!" She sat across the desk with anticipation. I opened the first letter, and out came a $4 check. I said: "There is the $4. Now we need the $90."

The next two envelopes did not contain any checks. However, the fifth envelope had a gift of $50! The next three were only letters, so there was just one left. Karen exclaimed, "There will have to be $40 in that envelope!"

I smiled as I slit open the top of the envelope and saw three checks inside. They had come from the Home Builders Class of the Wheaton Evangelical Free Church. I pulled out the first check and handed it to

Karen. It was for ten dollars. I then gave her the second check. It was also for ten dollars. After taking out the third check, I just looked at it. Her curiosity grew intense, and she said, "Well, how much?" I handed her the check for twenty dollars. She flopped back in her chair and said, "I don't believe it!" Years later, Karen got married. I sent her a wedding gift of $94.

The home was purchased, and the family moved in. One evening we were discussing the need to put an addition on the back of the house. We agreed that if God provided an initial $500, this would be our signal to proceed.

That very night, God prompted Marjorie Soderholm, a teacher at Trinity College, to write out a check for $500. She felt such a strong urgency to get it to us that she actually drove it down to the post office that night and put it in the outside mailbox!

When I was warned about the shotgun, it was not a joke. The man was very serious.

The Neighbor With the Shotgun

One Saturday morning after our radio broadcast, I was driving some young people home. As I turned north on Adams Road, I was impressed with the beauty of this country-like setting, and I said, "I sure would love to buy some property out here and have a training center for young people!"

From the back seat, I heard one of the young people, Juanita Turek, say: "My father wants to sell our

When I looked out at the open property in front of the house, I saw several horses in the field. The neighbor was breeding horses, and that was the reason why she became alarmed when any strangers who might disturb her horses would come by.

45

The original farmhouse is pictured above. I stood at the front door and watched as the shotgun peeked through the curtains of the window at the left. The gun was pointed at me for the first twenty minutes of our conversation.

The original building still stands. A front room and pillars were added to make it what it is today. The cement walk and railing of the original building are still inside the current one.

home. It is on five acres and has a big barn on it." Later I returned and talked to Mr. Turek. We agreed on a price, but he said: "Before you buy this property, you had better check with the woman across the road. She would not want any teenagers out here." I decided to walk over and talk to her. Before I left, Mr. Turek warned me, "She will probably run you off her property with a shotgun!" I stopped and prayed for protection and then walked across the road to her front door.

Birth of a Vision

When I knocked on the door, I heard a stern woman's voice demand, "Who are you, and what do you want?" I replied, "My name is Bill Gothard, and I would like to buy the property across the road, but I wanted to check with you first."

She replied, "Just a minute." She went over to her gun case, picked out a shotgun, and loaded it. Then she gave it to her twenty-eight-year-old daughter, who stuck its barrel through the curtains of a window and aimed it right at me! Then she slipped out the door and said, "Now, tell me again who you are and what you want!"

I explained that I had dedicated my life to work with young people, and I wanted to have a place where I could train them. She exclaimed, "How do you work with young people?!" As I described the work of teaching them the commands of Christ, she became interested and finally asked a startling question: "What is wrong with this property?"

I looked out over the beautiful twenty-acre estate with a small lake on it, surrounded by woods, and exclaimed, "Why, nothing!" To my total surprise, she stated: "When we get through using it we are going to give it away! Why don't we give it to you?" I thanked her in amazement and promised to keep in touch.

I made a point to stop in and visit her from time to time, always wondering if she were through using her property.

Death of a Vision

Finally she called me up one evening after eight years of waiting! She began by saying: "Bill, I know that I promised to give our property to you. However, we have been offered $125,000 for it, and we think we should sell it. Is there any way that you could match this offer?"

The amazing way that God provided the original twenty-acre Headquarters site is a powerful confirmation of Christ's command: "Give, and it shall be given unto you" (Luke 6:38). When I gave all of my money to God, He began providing for the work of His Kingdom.

In the early 1960s, that seemed like an astronomical amount of money and way above our ability to pay. I said, "We would not be able to pay that much money, so if you feel that you must sell the property, then I release you from your promise." She thanked me and we ended the conversation. Soon the property was sold to Phil Dressler, a builder, and Lou Main, a lawyer.

We were just beginning the Basic Seminar at that time, and the office in the recreation room of my home was becoming too small for the printing of materials and the management of the Seminar. So I called Lou Main and asked if they would be willing to sell the property. He responded: "Yes! We just decided to sell it!" I asked, "How much do you want for it?" He said, "Two hundred and sixty thousand dollars!" I was shocked and cautiously commented, "That is over twice what you paid for it just two years ago." He responded, "Yes, I know it is. However, we also know that it is worth more than that!"

Double Death of a Vision

Then Lou said, "Why don't you come over to my office and we will talk about it." This was a double death of my vision!

When I arrived at his office, he began the conversation by stating, "Now, I am not an atheist or anything like that, but how can you be so sure about God?" I answered, "There are many ways that I know the reality of God, but one that might be of greatest interest to you is how God provides funds for us in exact amounts on the day that they are needed!"

He stated, "Give me an example!" After I gave him an example, he said, "Give me another one!" We spent the next five hours rehearsing the supernatural ways that God had provided money in direct answer to prayer and without our letting anyone else know of the need.

Finally, Lou said: "Wait a minute! You have been telling me all these stories of how God has provided small amounts of money for you. How is He going to give you $260,000 to buy the land?"

I listened to the following words come out of my mouth: "We serve a big God. He is just as able to provide big amounts as little amounts."

Lou exclaimed, "If God gives you $260,000, even I will believe!" I silently thought to myself, "So will I!" The largest amount that we had ever received was the $10,000 from Dr. Ken Taylor.

The next week, I received a letter from a dentist in Seattle, Washington, Dr. Ken Murakami. He explained how the Basic Seminar had transformed his life and family and then informed me that they were selling property near Mt. Rainier and would be sending the money to the Institute for our ministry!

The amount that they were going to receive for their land was $260,000! I quickly drove over to the attorney's office and handed him the letter with the comment, "You might like to read this!" As he read it, his eyes got bigger, and he exclaimed, "I believe!"

He did not mean that he just believed that God had provided the exact amount. He was saying that he believed that Jesus truly was the Son of God, and He wants to be our Lord and Savior.

When it comes to planning for a harvest, it is not how much seed is in the farmer's bag that is important, but how much is in the ground. The same is true of a sower of money. "He which soweth sparingly shall reap also sparingly; and he which soweth bountifully shall reap also bountifully" (II Corinthians 9:6).

The Laws of the Harvest

1. We reap what we sow.

2. We reap where we sow.

3. We reap more than we sow.

4. We reap in a different season than we sow.

A Lesson From Harvest Laws

One of the most important lessons I have learned about money is that God compares it to a harvest. (See II Corinthians 9:6.) Just as there are precise laws that govern the growing of a crop, so God has established principles for wise stewardship of His finances.

One would think that after giving all of my money to God on two occasions and seeing His miraculous provision, I would have strong faith and not resort to trusting my own resources any more. However, it took one more painful lesson for me to learn this basic truth.

One morning as I got into my 1957 Chevy station wagon to go to a neighboring town, the thought came to me, "What if I have an accident today?"

I thought: "That was a strange idea! Why would I have such a thought?" So I said: "Lord, would you really cause me to have an accident? If so, what would be the reason?"

Immediately, a reason came to my mind. I had just started a third savings account as a special fund for personal pleasure items. At that moment, it had $318 in it. I had the silly idea that perhaps God would not notice this new bank account! Then I realized that if God removed His hand of protection from my life, all that money would be blown away like feathers out of my hand.

At the end of our street there was a line of stores with parallel parking in front. My accident-awakened mind reminded me that a car could quickly back out in front of me and I would crash into it. Therefore, I had better slow way down. I crept by that danger point and breathed a sigh of relief.

As I drove over a bridge, I saw in the distance the flashing red lights of a police car. I wondered what was happening. As I got closer, it became obvious that there had been an accident. A damaged car was on the side of the road.

I stared at the car as I drove by. When I looked back at the road, the car in front of me had come to a complete stop, and a policeman stood in front of it directing traffic. There was no way to stop. There was a terrible sound—my car crashing into his rear bumper.

Steam puffed out of my damaged radiator as I sat there in shock. Yet, I experienced a sense of warmth toward the Lord as Scripture came to my mind: "Whom the Lord loveth he chasteneth" (Hebrews 12:6).

The car was taken to a repair shop, and the amount of the repair bill was, yes, $318!

God wanted me to know that He was my best and only source of security and supply. Since then, I have never built a savings account—only a checking account to pay essential bills—and I give away the rest.

An Example of a "Refilled Bag"

So many times over the years, God has confirmed His promise to replenish my "seed" money if I give it away at His direction.

One day I toured a partially completed medical clinic for needy people in Romania. God prompted me to give a gift toward its completion. So I wrote a check for $5,000. As I gave it to the director, I said, "Please don't cash it until I return home and make sure I have that much in my checking account."

A sower in the New Testament differs from a "tither" in the Old Testament.

The tither gives 10% and keeps the rest. The sower gives God all of his assets and keeps only what he needs for living expenses. He tries to keep these minimal. God then provides for the basic needs of the sower, but God multiplies a sower's "sowing" account in ways that he never expected, so that he has more to give away.

"God is able to make all grace abound toward you; that ye, always having all sufficiency in all things, may abound to every good work" (II Corinthians 9:8).

> **"You can give without loving, but you cannot love without giving."**
> —Amy Carmichael

A few weeks later I received an unexpected personal gift from Rodger and Judy Gergeni, who have been directing our ministry at the Indianapolis Training Center for the past fourteen years. They had no knowledge of my gift, but they had been prompted by the Lord to give me a gift in the amount of $5,000!

Strengthening the Faith of Others

Church splits happen when members lose sight of the purpose for church. It is to be a gathering of believers who come together in one-accord power, which means that each one loves the Lord with all his heart, soul, mind, and strength. This produces a spirit of generosity as each one becomes a channel of love to the other. It is for this oneness that Jesus prayed: "That they may be one, even as we are one" (John 17:22).

When the distraught pastor of the Smyrna Baptist Church in Atlanta called to tell me that a church split was to occur on Sunday evening, I agreed to speak to the congregation before their vote.

On that Sunday night, the auditorium was packed, like it usually is for such an event. People who had not been there for years made it a point to show up. The atmosphere was filled with tension. The conflict was between the church and their Christian school.

Rather than taking one side or the other, I proposed a bigger plan that, if followed, would cause the church and school to become models for the nation. I offered to work with the pastor and headmaster to bring this plan about. The people caught a vision for what I was proposing, and they agreed to set aside their differences and work on a plan. That night we all got on our knees and brought resolution to the conflict.

During the Christmas break, I brought the pastor, headmaster, and several student leaders to our Oak Brook Headquarters to work out the plan. I mentioned that the plan would cost about $50,000 and that we would pay for it since the school and church were on a tight budget.

At the next break, I walked into my office, and several student council officers followed me. A small stack of mail was on my desk. The student council president had heard me tell about how God had provided our funds in answer to prayer and often to the exact dollar. So he said excitedly, "Let's open your mail."

As we opened each envelope, there were various letters. However, one contained a check. He picked it up. His eyes got big, and he exclaimed: "Fifty thousand dollars!! Now I have seen with my own eyes how God provides money in exact amounts firsthand!" That really was a provision from the Lord, because we do not ordinarily receive checks of that nature.

Since I do not ask for money, every envelope is a surprise from God, whether it contains money, a testimony of a transformed life, or requests for help.

The Far-Reaching Impact of a Precise Gift

When our printing needs increased beyond the capacity of a small press, we began looking for a five-color Heidelberg press. After much searching and negotiating, we were ready to bring our report to the Board. The price of the press was $300,000. The night before the Board meeting, we received a letter

from a Chinese man in California whom we had never met. Inside the envelope was a check for $300,000.

Every time we give a tour through our printing department, we show people the press and tell them the story behind it. When one leader heard the account, he burst out with this exclamation: "Praise God!" This is an amazing response from a Buddhist.

Another leader from Russia was given the tour. He was a member of the Parliament and made it clear to us that he was a Communist. When he heard of God's precise provision, he exclaimed: "This is amazing! We need this in Russia! Wait till I tell President Yeltsin about it."

A factor that makes this report even more significant is that the press was to be used to print materials for other nations, especially Taiwan. To have an unknown Chinese man send in the exact amount on the day it was needed was like the Lord sending in His final count of confirmation.

HEALTH

. . . is not treating symptoms, but identifying and resolving the stresses that cause sicknesses and diseases and then helping the body heal itself.

3

The Way to TOTAL HEALTH:

Resolve All Your Stresses!

One of my fervent prayers for many years was that God would reveal the real causes and cures of sicknesses and diseases. Amazingly, this prayer is being answered through a deeper understanding of the commands of Christ!

This should not be surprising, because Jesus is the Great Physician and His ministry was all about healing— the healing of the spirit, soul, and body. He has also promised to make Himself known to those who keep His commands. (See John 14:21.)

What Is Total Health?

Total health begins by understanding that we were created as one being with three distinct parts: the spirit, the soul, and the body.

The spirit is the "home" of faith, wisdom, discernment, conscience, genuine love, joy, peace, etc. The soul is the center of the intellect, emotions, and will. The body contains our physical senses, including taste, touch, sight, sound, and smell.

Just as there are laws that govern the universe, so there are laws that govern the health of our body.

Sickness
is a condition that with proper care and time will get better.

Disease
is a condition that regardless of care will get worse.

Total health is determined by how we resolve the stresses of our soul.

SPIRIT
The Home of:

- **Faith**
- **Wisdom**
- **Love**
- **Conscience**

SOUL
The Home of:

- **Intellect**
- **Emotions**
- **Will**

BODY
The Home of:

- **Taste**
- **Touch**
- **Sight**
- **Sound**
- **Smell**

Total health is experienced when our spirit is in fellowship with God's Spirit, our soul is functioning in accordance with the commands of Christ, and our body is under the control of our spirit and soul.

I used to assume that I was a body that had a spirit and a soul. Then one day I realized that I am actually a spirit in a body that also has a soul. This explains to me what happened in the Garden of Eden. God revealed Himself as a God of love, which then demanded that we have the ability to make choices. Love requires a choice.

Adam and Eve chose to reject God by putting their intellect above His Word. Their *soul* and *body* continued to live for a time, but the real person of their *spirit* experienced what God predicted: "In the day that thou eatest thereof thou shalt surely die" (Genesis 2:17). Their fellowship with God was broken, and they began to experience the stresses that result in sicknesses, diseases, and death.

Unfortunately, Adam and Eve passed their fallen nature to all of their descendants. Thus, we were all born "spiritually dead." We do not have the fellowship with God that we need. This emptiness motivates us to search for a genuine relationship with Him.

My Search for God

I will never forget my futile attempts to be good enough to earn God's gift of eternal life. One morning I woke up and decided: "Today, I will not say or do anything wrong!" By the end of that day, I had realized that I had done more bad things than normal!

This did not alarm me, because I purposed to try harder the next day. However, that day was even worse! Then I had this horrifying thought: "If God put all of my bad days on one side of His scale, and all of my good days on the other side, there is no way that I would ever get into heaven!"

A few days later, my mother told me that a Child Evangelism Fellowship Bible Club was being held in a vacant store building at the end of our block. She encouraged me to attend it. The teacher was Virginia Stevens. She told the stories of the Bible with such practical detail and application that I felt like I was there with the characters.

She began, "Today, we are going to talk about Abraham." Then she asked, "Does anyone know who he was?" I quickly raised my hand and she called on me. I said, "Abraham Lincoln!" I did not understand the laughter of the other children. However, the teacher recognized my lack of Biblical knowledge and graciously smoothed over my answer.

The vacant annex of this building was the location of the Bible club where I first heard the Gospel.

It was during that session that I learned how to be "reborn" in my spirit. That night I knelt in my bedroom, told God that I needed His salvation, and asked Jesus to come into my life, cleanse me of all my sin, and make me His child.

The next morning I experienced some of the initial evidences of being "born again." Even though I was a poor reader, I had a new desire to read and understand the Bible. I also experienced a new love for God and a desire to be like Jesus. I had a greater awareness of right and wrong, and I wanted to tell as many others as I could about the life that I had just discovered.

I realized that if God placed all of my bad days on one side of His scale and all of my good days on the other side, there was no way I would ever be good enough to go to heaven. God affirms this: "There is none righteous, no, not one" (Romans 3:10).

I soon realized, however, that although my spirit was now "born again," my soul still had a lot of need for change. It is only as our mind, will, and emotions are transformed by the commands of Christ that we will experience inward peace and total health. Thus, John wrote, "I wish above all things that thou mayest prosper and be in health, even [in the same way] as thy soul prospereth" (III John 2).

"All we like sheep have gone astray; we have turned every one to his own way" (Isaiah 53:6).

57

When Jesus tried to explain the new birth to a religious leader named Nicodemus, the leader said: "How can a man be born when he is old? can he enter the second time into his mother's womb, and be born?" (John 3:4).

Jesus then reminded him of Moses lifting up a brass snake on a pole in the wilderness so that anyone who had been bitten by a poisonous snake could be healed by looking in faith at the snake. The snake was a symbol of Jesus, Who took upon Himself all of our sin so that "whosoever shall call upon the name of the Lord shall be saved" (Romans 10:13).

Relating Stresses to Diseases

A few years ago I learned about a doctor whose son had been killed. The doctor could not overcome his grief and bitterness, and soon he developed cancer.

He wondered if there was a relationship between his bitterness and his cancer, so he carried out an extensive study with twenty thousand patients. He found that there was a direct correlation between stress and diseases, but when he showed his research to the university that gave him his degree, they refused to examine it.

When I heard about this, I thought, "If that doctor is correct, his conclusions will be in the Bible, because God's Word is our 'handbook' on health."

I began my search with the marvelous Sermon on the Mount, found in Matthew 5, 6, and 7. This was the first major message that Jesus gave to the crowds who followed Him. It was so powerful and rich with wisdom and application that when He finished, the crowds were astonished because He spoke as one with authority. In that awesome discourse I now saw seven specific stresses. They are as follows:

1. **Anger**—*including frustration and irritation*
2. **Guilt**—*reflected in blame and anxiety*
3. **Lust**—*unrestrained passions and addictions*
4. **Bitterness**—*involving hatred and revenge*
5. **Greed**—*for money, possessions, or power*
6. **Fear**—*of rejection, failure, and the future*
7. **Envy**—*expressed in desiring what others have*

After seeing this list of stresses, I remembered that there are seven primary systems in our body. I wondered if there was any relationship between our stresses and these body systems. The result of checking this out scientifically and Biblically was amazing!

1. **Anger**—*affects the cardiovascular system*

2. **Guilt**—*affects the nervous system*

3. **Lust**—*affects the endocrine system*

4. **Bitterness**—*affects the digestive system*

5. **Greed**—*affects the immune system*

6. **Fear**—*affects the respiratory system*

7. **Envy**—*affects the musculoskeletal system*

When a doctor in Texas saw this relationship between stresses and diseases, he tested it out on his patients. First, he would have them circle the stress that troubled them the most, and then he would ask them to describe their ailments. He found that the results were 90% accurate in linking their stress with their disease.

Even more significant is the growing number of people who are experiencing freedom from sicknesses and diseases as soon as they identify and resolve the underlying stresses that caused them.

Chronic Stomach Pain Caused by Bitterness

For two and a half years, Theresa Apple was in constant pain. She went to doctor after doctor seeking relief.

Our Potential Life Span

Dr. Alexis Carrel

Dr. Carrel was awarded the Nobel Prize for keeping tissues of a chicken heart alive for many years, thus suggesting that cells could remain alive indefinitely. Dr. Carrel immersed the cells in a solution of electrolyte nutrients. The solution was changed daily. The average life span of a chicken is seven years. However, these cells continued to live and remain healthy until the researchers stopped replacing the nutrients thirty-four years later, two years after the death of Dr. Carrel.

When Adam and Eve sinned, the potential of an indefinite life span ended. Every person is in the process of dying. The goal is to extend our life as long as possible by obeying God's laws.

Five Causes of Diseases

1. What we think
The lies and fears that we have will directly affect our health.

2. What we say
"Death and life are in the power of the tongue" (Proverbs 18:21).

3. What we do
"He that soweth to his flesh shall of the flesh reap corruption; but he that soweth to the Spirit shall of the Spirit reap life everlasting" (Galatians 6:8).

4. What we eat
Nutrition is important but not as vital as the above three factors. Good food will become toxic in a bitter environment. Thus, Solomon stated, "Better is a dinner of herbs where love is, than a stalled ox and hatred therewith" (Proverbs 15:17).

5. What we inherit
The mental, emotional, and physical weaknesses of our forefathers are passed on to us. However, we can establish disciplines to keep them from damaging our health.

They gave her batteries of tests, prescribed many drugs, and had her go through an operation that doctors assured her would solve the problem. Nothing worked! She only grew worse.

Before every meal she would take fifteen pills. At night, she would get only one or two hours of sleep—if she propped her head 2 feet above her pillow and put a heating pad on her back.

Theresa and her husband attended one of our Total Health Seminars. I sat down at their breakfast table and asked Theresa how she was feeling. That is when she explained the factors given above.

I asked Theresa what had happened two and a half years earlier, and she described the brutal beating of her father-in-law by a youth gang. She had made heroic efforts to care for him in order to nurse him back to health.

The day before her father-in-law was to be released to her care at home, a hospital nurse gave him the wrong medication, and he went into a vegetative state. Soon he died. Theresa held deep bitterness toward that youth gang for their attacks, the nurse for her misjudgment, and several others who were connected with this incident.

During the next twenty minutes, I was able to help her see what had happened from a whole new perspective. As soon as she understood and accepted these Biblical concepts, her pain stopped. At the next meal, she did not feel that she needed her pills, and that night she had her first good night's sleep in two and a half years—lying flat on her bed.

Our conversation took place many years ago, and there has been no return of her chronic stomach pain!

Osteoporosis Caused by Envy

Lisa was committed to good nutrition and providing healthy meals for her family. She studied materials on health and took many kinds of supplements. In spite of all this, she had chronic fatigue, her weight began to drop until she weighed just 95 pounds, her cholesterol count went up, and her doctors informed her that she had only 64% of her bone mass left!

When Lisa learned that osteoporosis may be caused by envy, she did not think that this would apply to her. She had a loving husband, obedient and productive children, a new debt-free home in the country, and a happy life. Yet, she could not explain her condition. She reread the manual titled *How to Resolve Seven Deadly Stresses*. This time, she saw the problem. She was not envying another woman, but instead she was envying an ideal that her husband was not measuring up to.

When Lisa confessed this envy to the Lord and asked her husband to forgive her, the stress vanished. With the stress of envy resolved, she found a high-quality nutritional product that began to help her body heal itself. Today she has no chronic fatigue, her weight is normal, her cholesterol count is normal, and her bone density is also near 100%!

A Breathing Disorder Caused by Fear

Oksana was sixteen years old when she and her father visited IBLP Headquarters. When I met her, I asked, "How are you feeling?" She answered, "Not good."

Bitterness has a direct effect on the digestive tract. If the digestive tract were to be stretched out, it would have a surface the size of a tennis court! It provides the primary defense against toxins and infections. Sixty percent of the immune system and more than 80% of immune antibody-producing cells are located within the inner lining of the digestive tract. This system is also an intelligence center, along with the brain and heart. It contains 100 million neuro-transmitters, which is the same number as are in our brain. It stores data that will cause inflammation that can trigger immune disorders.

The fear of death holds people in bondage all their lifetime and is broken only as we receive the life of Christ.
(See Hebrews 2:15.)

A clear association between asthma and the fear of abandonment has been established in many studies. Asthma among children from single-parent homes is twice as prevalent as it is in children from two-parent homes. The condition of asthma is a hypersensitive state of the airways associated with an imbalance in the immune system and the nervous system.

She then explained that she could not breathe through her nose and that her circulation was very poor. Therefore, her hands and feet were always cold. The doctors had prescribed inhalers. However, they had caused side effects. Sometimes, she would get so weak that she would faint.

I explained that breathing disorders often are caused by fear of abandonment, and I asked Oksana if she ever had that fear. "Oh, yes!" she replied. "I often dream that my father will die." Every night during the previous week, she had experienced one of these nightmares.

Oksana had built her security around her earthly father. My goal was to help her transfer that security to her heavenly Father, Who promises His children that He will never leave them or forsake them. I used some of the commands of Christ to help her understand how to make this transfer. The next day her breathing disorder cleared up. There was no more need for her inhalers, and her hands and feet were no longer cold.

How Commands Relate to Health

One day the thought came to me, "Why don't you match the commands of Christ with the seven stresses?" I took out a bookmark that listed all forty-nine commands and matched each one with the most appropriate stress. I noticed that there were seven commands for each stress.

If these commands were lived out, the stress would clear up. This gave a whole new excitement and motivation to learn and apply Christ's commands. They are actually practical ways to apply God's truth and love. Also, by carrying out a command of Christ, we develop a related, positive character quality. Thus, we have seven stresses, seven body systems, and for each stress, seven commands and seven character qualities.

The Command to Receive God's Power

We do not have the ability to live out the commands of Christ. Our best efforts will only end in failure, disillusionment, or pride of partial achievement.

When I was born again, I received the indwelling power of God's Spirit in my spirit. (See John 3:3–6.) God speaks of this as a "down payment" of the greater power that He wants to give every believer. (See II Corinthians 1:22.)

That greater power involves engrafting the Word of God into our soul as Scripture states: "Wherefore lay apart all filthiness and superfluity of naughtiness, and receive with meekness the engrafted word, which is able to save your souls" (James 1:21).

However, Scripture also speaks of special enablement that comes by the laying on of hands. Paul received this empowerment when Ananias laid hands on him, and Paul passed that on to Timothy in the same way. Thus, Paul wrote, "Stir up the gift of God, which is in thee by the putting on of my hands. For God hath not given us the spirit of fear; but of power, and of love, and of a sound mind" (II Timothy 1:6–7).

I was amazed one day to see that this Biblical procedure is a foundational principle for every believer. (See Hebrews 6:1.) Therefore, I asked my pastor if he and the church elders would lay hands on me and ask God to increase His blessing on the ministry that God has entrusted to me. Since that day, I have experienced a new measure of God's power.

The foundation stone of a building is significant because every other stone is set in reference to it. If the cornerstone is off, the entire building will be skewed. Therefore, when God states that the laying on of hands is a part of the foundation of the Gospel of Christ, it is very significant: "Let us go on unto perfection; not laying again the foundation of repentance from dead works, and of faith toward God, of the doctrine of baptisms, and of laying on of hands" (Hebrews 6:1–2).

At **salvation**, the Holy Spirit indwells our **spirit**.

As we **grow** in Christ, the Holy Spirit fills our **soul**.

As we **yield** our **bodily members** to God's Spirit, He controls them. (See Romans 6–8.)

63

Brittany is enrolled in our Verity Institute, which helps students earn a fully accredited bachelor of arts degree in only two years.

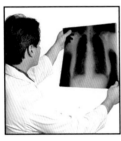

When friends learned about Brittany's healing, they wanted to know if she had any X-rays of her condition before and after. So she went down to her chiropractor and had a new set taken. When he compared them with earlier X-rays, he exclaimed: "This is amazing! What chiropractor did you go to in Chicago to get this result?" She was able to explain that she had gone to the best Physican in the universe.

Kyphosis Caused by Bad Posture

As Brittany was walking out of my office, I called out to her, "Brittany!" She turned and I asked, "Did your mother ever tell you to stand up straight?" She laughed, saying: "Yes, for years, but now I have continual pain in my back and shoulders, and it is even worse when I try to stand up straight. When I turned eighteen, my chiropractor told me that my condition was irreversible, and when I am fifty, I will be hunched way over when I walk."

I then asked, "Would you like this condition to be corrected?" She said, "Yes, I certainly would!" I called George Mattix, an ordained elder on my staff, to join me in carrying out a Biblical procedure that is described in James 5:14–16. After the prayer, Brittany felt a weight upon her shoulders. That night, there was a strange cracking of the bones, which happened even though she was not moving.

During the night, Brittany woke up four times due to the pain of her bones "popping." The fourth time, she felt a sense of healing and peace and had a deep sleep.

When she woke up in the morning, her back was completely free of pain and muscle tightness. She was able to stand up straight with no discomfort. The Lord had been her Divine Physician that night, putting all her bones, muscles, and ligaments back in place.

Every day she is rejoicing in the total healing that she has received and the awareness of God's power and love in and through her for ministry.

Musculoskeletal Pain Caused by Envy

Dr. Alan Sivells is a pastor, master carpenter, and father of thirteen children. Several years ago he attended one of our Total Health Seminars. During a break he came up to me and explained the reasons why he was there. He was experiencing severe headaches and shoulder pains. The pain was so intense that he was not able to lift his hands above his shoulders, and he often had to have his wife help him get dressed in the morning.

This condition was obviously a great hindrance to his work as a carpenter and his ability to concentrate on his studies as a pastor. When he heard the verse that says "envy [is] the rottenness of the bones" (Proverbs 14:30), he made a further study of envy in Scripture. He also was convicted by Proverbs 27:4: "Wrath is cruel, and anger is outrageous; but who is able to stand before envy?"

After his study, the Lord convicted him of an area of envy. He confessed it as sin and asked for forgiveness and cleansing.

Here is his written report: "At a Total Health Seminar, I learned about the relationship between the musculoskeletal system and envy. I did not think that this applied to me until I realized that there was one area of envy that I had. I cleared it up and also began to follow the practice of electrolyte balance. Nine days later, I felt completely well. I even played football for two hours with my boys, throwing overhand passes."

In addition to granting physical healing, God has marvelously blessed his marriage, family, and ministry.

The Purpose of Healing

When someone requests prayer for the healing of a serious disease, I usually will ask, "What important goals do you have to carry out for God's Kingdom?" This is often a new thought. Most people want to be healed so they can continue in their self-centered plans and pleasures. In Scripture, we are told that those who are sick are to call for the elders of the church and be anointed with oil, and the prayer of faith saves the sick.
(See James 5:14–16.)

Just as David and others were anointed for important ministries, so anointing for healing should be done in order to carry out great works in God's Kingdom. After Dr. Sivells was healed, his family and church experienced revival.

The Next Chapter in an Amazing Story

The world will long remember what happened on September 11, 2001. Most people will remember that date for the horrific terrorist attacks against the Pentagon and the World Trade Centers, which claimed thousands of innocent lives. Anna will remember the day for another reason. On that very day, she walked into a medical clinic and began treatment for a deadly cancer that had invaded her body.

When *The Power of Crying Out* was published in 2002, the lead article was the story of Anna. The chances of her survival had been almost nonexistent. Yet, the Headquarters staff and others cried out for her healing, and God heard our cry. After Anna was healed, her doctor, Stephen Ayre, M.D., came to Headquarters and said to the staff: "I want to make it clear that the healing that you see in Anna is not the result of my treatment. It is truly a miracle of God."

The oldest daughter of ten children in a single-parent home, Anna began experiencing excruciating pain in her hip early in August. On September 11, while the world reeled over the news of the attack on America, Anna began chemotherapy for Hodgkin's lymphoma, which had spread to her bones.

The doctor recommended a treatment plan, but prospects were not at all hopeful. Anna struggled with side effects from several pain medications, including morphine. Her weight had plunged, and she experienced so much pain that she needed assistance just to walk across the room. Her cancer was so far advanced that there was little likelihood of turning it back.

Anna had worked on the Headquarters staff for the Institute in Basic Life Principles. She had also spent time in Romania, serving students and orphans in that nation.

Anna and her brother served in Romania on a team like the one pictured above. This was further motivation for us to cry out for her healing and ministry for the Lord.

Stunned and grieved by the shocking turn of events in her young life, Anna called for her church elders to anoint her and pray for her. The Headquarters staff was also deeply concerned. Gathering as a staff, we cried aloud to the Lord: "O Lord, Abba Father, deliver Anna from cancer and raise her up for your glory in the name of Jesus!"

On Christmas Day, Anna recalled the account of the widow pleading her case before the unjust judge. (See Luke 18:1–8.) She spent the day crying out to God.

Two days later, she and her mother returned to the doctor. After reviewing the tests used to monitor the cancer, the astounded oncologist declared that she was cancer free! According to the tests, there was no trace left of an aggressive cancer that already had reached stage 4B, the final stage before death. Soon after that appointment, Anna returned to the ski slopes!

Anna married Glenn Kinsey and now has twin boys, Wesley and Walker.

The Miracle Twins

Miracle twins

Anna explains the medical impossibility of her having any children in the following report: "My twins are miracles from God, because I was told by several doctors that I could not have any children. I had no cycle, and I had gone through menopause.

"I had done loads of chemotherapy, which had destroyed my reproductive system. Seven years' worth of chemo was given to me in only five days! At the University of Michigan, I was told that I had more cancer in my body than anyone the doctor had ever seen."

The words of God are certainly true: "I am the LORD, the God of all flesh: is there any thing too hard for me?" (Jeremiah 32:27).

How to Resolve 7 Deadly Stresses contains a wealth of information about how stress can be directly related to disease and how it can be resolved by the commands of Christ. For more information, visit lifepurposehealth.com.

Transforming Painful Memories

One of the major keys to resolving stress is to transform painful memories into powerful reminders of God's truth. It is this truth that will set us free.

During a conference for Romanian medical officials that was held at IBLP Headquarters, one of them leaned over the table and said to me: "Bill, you mentioned the importance of transforming painful memories. I have one. Could you help me transform it?"

I asked her for the details, and she explained that her seventy-two-year-old father had suffered from a heart condition that she had believed could be improved through an operation. However, when Carmen had told her mother about her plans, her mother had appealed to her not to do it.

Then one night Carmen had a terrifying dream. She dreamed that her father was lying in a hospital bed with no blood in him. For three nights in a row she had the same nightmare.

The operation took place on a Friday. The following Sunday at 3 P.M., while the hospital surgeons were absent, a section of her father's descending aorta ruptured, causing all the blood to flow out of his body, resulting in his death.

Immediately Carmen's mother accused her of "killing" her father, which she vigorously denied. Nevertheless, she grieved over what had happened, and for the last five years she had been in a state of depression, which she treated with medications. How could such a painful memory be transformed?

Finding Freedom With a New Perspective

Without intending to, Carmen had placed her intellect above the Word of God. Scripture commands

When Carmen shared her painful memory, no one else knew about the details except her mother. However, once the memory was transformed, she was excited about telling other people about it. This eagerness to share a new perspective of a past failure is significant evidence that a memory has been transformed.

Every experience we have ever had is stored in the limbic system of our brain. This system attaches an emotion to each memory. If it is positive, it will strengthen our immune system. If it is negative, it will damage our immune system and upset our hormonal balance.

68

us to honor our father and our mother and to not forsake the counsel of our father or mother when they are older. These Scriptures were violated.

I pointed out to Carmen, "For five years, you have been trying to convince yourself that you are not guilty of what your mother is accusing you of, yet you know deep down in your heart that your mother's warnings should have been followed. You rejected her counsel, and you are now grieving over the consequences."

At that point, I gave her a new way of looking at her situation with Biblical concepts that she had never heard before. These made sense to her, and she grasped on to them. As a result, she was able to see her situation from an entirely new perspective, and the depression left her.

The next morning she had a whole new freedom and excitement. She told me that she had just shared with a relative about our conversation the previous night. Not only were her painful memories transformed, but she now was excited about telling other people exactly how those memories had been transformed so that she could help them deal with similar painful memories.

There was no longer a need to treat depression, and she now has a new basis for helping other people gain total health.

A Deeper Significance

I asked Carmen what benefits had come from her painful experience, and she said, "It brought me to salvation, because before this happened I had no room for God in my life."

Immediately I thought of an analogy and I said to her: "Isn't this significant? Jesus shed His blood to provide salvation for you, and your father shed his blood to bring you to that salvation." This analogy had immediate significance to Carmen, and she has enjoyed sharing it with others.

These medical officials have major areas of responsibility in Romania. After hearing about the importance of resolving stress before trying to treat symptoms, they signed a declaration that they would take this approach to their nation.

JOY

. . . is not based on the
praise we receive but on the
powerful truths we discover
from being reviled.

4

The Way to
GREAT JOY:

Enjoy Rewards for Being Reviled!

On February 2, 1952, at 10:50 in the morning, the door of my third-period class burst open and a student aid from the main office rushed in and handed my teacher a green slip.

A green slip meant that whoever received it was in real trouble! The teacher looked at the slip, looked at me, and then said, "Bill Gothard, this is for you!" Fellow students exclaimed, "Bill, what did you do?!"

I looked at the green slip and noticed that it had been signed by the school principal and the school superintendent! I could not miss the exclamation mark after the word "Now!"

When I arrived at the main office, I was ushered into the superintendent's office. There were four people seated on one side and an empty seat for me on the other side of the room.

The superintendent got right to the point. In a tone filled with restrained emotion, he

Up to 120 students would meet in my home nearly every Tuesday evening during my four years of high school. This made the principal very nervous.

The day of confrontation

71

"Blessed are they which are persecuted for righteousness' sake: for theirs is the kingdom of heaven. Blessed are ye, when men shall revile you, and persecute you, and shall say all manner of evil against you falsely, for my sake.

"Rejoice, and be exceeding glad: for great is your reward in heaven: for so persecuted they the prophets which were before you" (Matthew 5:10–12).

The rewards in heaven come from the greater fruit that God gives as a direct result of our being reviled on earth.

said, "Bill Gothard, are you running a prayer meeting in this school?" I wondered how to answer.

A few days earlier about twenty young people had asked to meet in the cafeteria before school to encourage each other for the day. On that morning, two other students had joined our group, and when they heard the Gospel, they both received Christ as their Savior. So we all had bowed our heads in prayer as they prayed to receive Christ.

During their prayer, I happened to look up at the cafeteria doors. I saw the heads of two teachers go by the little window in the door; then they backed up and looked at our group with wide eyes. No doubt, they had informed the superintendent of what was happening. I did not think the superintendent wanted all of this explanation, so I simply said, "Yes, sir."

The superintendent's emotion increased as he said: "I know what you are trying to do. You are trying to convert the whole school to your religion, aren't you?" I tried to explain that my goal was to help fellow students experience a relationship like I had with Jesus Christ, not to convert them to a religion. His fervor increased as he said, "I know that I cannot stop you from meeting on public property for peaceable purposes, but if you do not stop your prayer meetings, I am going to send a letter to every family in this town, telling them what I think of your program."

I assured him that it was not my intention to create a problem and that I would move our meetings to some other place. This, however, did not satisfy him.

The next week, a member of the student council informed me that the superintendent had called a group of the most popular students into his office and warned them not to be involved with the programs in my home or with me. Word quickly spread through the school. However, I continued to find creative ways to share the Gospel with each student every year.

One year I sent a birthday card to each student with the following message: "Happy birthday! The greatest gift I could give you is news on how to have a second birthday—by being born again."

The next year I conducted telephone surveys, asking students what they thought was the most important thing in life and then sending a little booklet which explained that the greatest thing in life was a personal relationship with Jesus Christ.

This science award was a further demonstration of God honoring the meditation on Scripture that I was carrying out during my high school and college years.

God Writes Last Chapters

In 1953 God arranged for an unexpected event that was to involve the entire student body. An official from the Future Scientists of America Foundation

called the superintendent and said to him: "We are pleased to inform you that one of your students has won a high honor in a Future Scientists of America contest, and we would like to present your school with a plaque. Would you be able to arrange for this?"

Eager for the encouragement that this would bring to the school, the superintendent arranged for a school-wide assembly and then discovered who the winning student was. I can only imagine how he must have felt, coming before all of the students and giving a tribute to me for winning that award.

Word spread that the superintendent was not happy with my witness on the campus. As the student body filed into the auditorium, this made it all the more stunning when he, along with the official from the Future Scientists of America Foundation, called me to the podium and gave some words of praise.

73

At graduation, fellow students gave an unexpected expression of appreciation for my investment in their lives.

In my senior year of high school, my classmates voted to give a scholarship of appreciation to one graduating fellow and girl from our class of more than four hundred. During the ceremony, the superintendent called out my name for me to come up and receive that unexpected gift.

Out of all of the events conducted during my four years in high school, I was able to attend only part of one football game. However, my classmates knew that I was committed to helping them in their personal lives.

Since the age of fifteen, it has been my life goal to work with high schoolers.

As a freshman, I was given a half-hour of free radio time over WTAQ. The radio program continued for the next nine years and also aired over WMBI of Chicago.

God's Way to Honor— Humility

During the next six years of college and graduate school, the number-one passion of my life was to work with teenagers. This involved presenting scenic chalk-talks for youth groups throughout Chicago and its suburbs, overseeing eighteen high school Bible clubs, and producing a half-hour radio program each week.

In my college classes, I took two sets of notes. One was for the course, and the other was for my youth work. During the lunch periods I would recruit the most outstanding students that I could find to be counselors in the Bible clubs. By the end of the year, I had over ninety.

By the time I was twenty-nine years old, I was responsible for the Bible clubs in sixty-five high schools in Chicago and the surrounding suburbs. As far as I was concerned, this would be my life work. But God had other plans for me and an unexpected way to achieve them.

One day I was in my office at 107 North Dearborn in Chicago when a new staff member strode in and announced to me, "Bill, all of us on the staff think that you are proud!"

I did not realize that a movement to replace me as the director was well under way. I assured the staff member that I certainly could acknowledge pride, and I thanked her for bringing it to my attention.

When she left, I made a list of the people whom I had offended and asked each one if he or she would forgive me for my offensive attitudes of pride.

One offended person was a twenty-one-year-old

Following the Second World War, there was a surge of interest in knowing God and His way of life. More than 100,000 people filled Soldiers Field in Chicago for a rally, and Christian clubs started up in high schools throughout the nation, including the Chicago area.

The Bible Club movement in Chicago was named "Hi-C Clubs" and spread throughout sixty-five campuses around Chicago and its suburbs. It was organized by the Christian Teachers' Association of Chicago and held weekly meetings. I became the director of this organization when I was twenty-nine years old.

fellow whom I had hired during the previous summer. One day I asked him if he was going to be at a staff meeting, and he said, "No, I think that I want to go fishing that day!"

I asked him to come with me for a ride and a talk. During our talk I asked: "Let's suppose that you were sent out by a mission board to a certain country and told to stay on the coast. However, you firmly believed that it was God's will for you to go into the interior of that country. What would you do?"

God gave Joseph a vision of future greatness. However, first Joseph had to go through a humbling process. His brothers reviled him and called him a "dreamer."

The hatred and rejection that Joseph received from his brothers were the very factors that allowed Joseph to fulfill his vision. Later Joseph stated to his brothers, "As for you, ye thought evil against me; but God meant it unto good, to bring to pass, as it is this day, to save much people alive" (Genesis 50:20).

He quickly responded, "I would obey God and go to the interior!" I replied, "That would be a wrong decision, because if God led you into the mission organization through that board, He would lead you while you were in it through that board. If God wanted to change your direction, He would change the mind of the board or lead you out of the organization." The young man did not say a word, but a week later he quit. Little did I realize that soon I would be demonstrating that little talk that I had given to him.

When I called up a board member and asked him to forgive me for my pride, he burst out weeping! I was shocked! He replied, "Bill, I will forgive you, but I am still going to do what I have planned to do."

A few days later I found out what he had planned to do. He called together a special meeting with the staff and the board. I was not invited. A list of ten grievances was given to the board, and they sent a representative to inform me that I had been removed as the director. They wanted me to stay on staff but not as the one in charge.

I asked what the grievances were, since I thought that I had cleared them all up. Several days later, they gave me the list. I was shocked! They were all minor issues, like a discrepancy over the actual number of clubs that we had or personal convictions like not taking a salary so that we would not have to ask for money. The more I tried to explain, the more resistance they gave me.

Soon, they appointed a new director. I was stunned! It was the twenty-one-year-old freshman in Bible Institute who had quit the previous year! Now he was the director, and I had to report to him. He seemed to enjoy this new relationship.

I found great comfort by reading the Psalms and also Lamentations 3:27–31: "It is good for a man that he bear the yoke in his youth. He sitteth alone and keepeth silence, because he hath borne it upon him. He putteth his mouth in the dust; if so be there may be hope. He giveth his cheek to him that smiteth him: he is filled full with reproach. For the Lord will not cast off forever."

My original life goal of working with the youth of Chicago was what I had decided would be the best way I could advance God's Kingdom and do damage to Satan's kingdom.

The humbling process was not yet over. The board told me to figure out what I wanted to do, because they did not know how to direct my activities.

Later, I proposed a plan that I knew would work. It involved forming teams of young people on high school campuses and teaching them how to achieve steps to spiritual maturity, such as thanking God for the way He designed them, learning how to honor their parents, gaining a clear conscience, forgiving those who had offended them, yielding their rights, and meditating on Scripture.

The plan that I presented to the board of that youth organization was actually the content of my master's degree thesis. After fifteen years of working with youth, I believed that it was the best way to help them grow in their walk with the Lord.

The board members stared at me as I excitedly explained this proposal. They looked at each other. Finally, one stated, "I would not give you a plugged nickel for this plan!" He was the president of a Christian teachers' association. Then the dean of the local Bible Institute spoke: "This is obviously a work of the flesh!" I just sat there in amazement.

Finally, another board member spoke: "Bill, if you are so sure that this is a good plan, why don't you go out and try it for a year and then come back and tell us how it worked!" I agreed to do this.

When Joseph was falsely accused of an immoral action by Potiphar's wife and put in prison, he could have been totally discouraged. Instead, he had no bitterness or blame but cheered up his fellow prisoners by his strong faith in God's promises.

We see a pattern in the way that God deals with us. As in the case of Joseph, if God allows a bad report to get out, He will overtake it with a good report. On this basis I said, "Let the bad report go as far as it can, because then the good report will go farther." This came about with the amazing growth of the Basic Seminar.

From Being Reviled to Rejoicing

After being reviled, replaced, and rejected, it seemed like my whole world had come crashing down upon me. Everything for which I had sacrificed, worked, and planned had been taken away from me. In its place was a damaged reputation. During that critical time, God gave me the following steps of action:

1. Review God's Vision for My Life

When everything seemed to go wrong, I had to ask myself, "Did God really call me to dedicate my life to reach young people?" The answer was a resounding "Yes!" Whenever I saw a group of young people, my heart would leap for joy.

2. Trade in My Reputation for God's

My first thoughts after being reviled and replaced were "What will people think of me?" and "How will I explain what happened so they will not condemn me?" I realized then that God did not really care about what people thought about me. He was only concerned that people saw Christ in my actions and attitudes.

I said: "Lord, I now give you my reputation. It is no longer important what people think of me. It is only important that I am properly representing You. If people love You, they should then love me. If, however, they hate You, I will expect them to hate me also." That outlook gave me a great freedom.

3. Learn Why God Let It Happen

God uses the wrath of people to carry out His larger plans. He is also a God of cause and effect. Bad things do not "just happen" to us. When I asked God why He let all these calamities come upon me, He reminded me of a vow I had made when I was in high school. I had vowed that I would talk to an average of three people a day about the Lord. I was able to carry it out during high school, but then I got so busy that I did not continue it.

Now that God had released me from all of my busyness as the director, I was free to catch up on my vow. It was this realization that motivated me to go out on the streets of Chicago neighborhoods and look for youth gangs. For the next eight months I traveled to different parts of the city in the evenings and established friendships with youth groups.

My first challenge was to make a meaningful contact with a youth gang. As I walked up to them they would all stare at me and wonder what I wanted. I began by asking, "Do you fellows live in the neighborhood?" They usually replied by saying: "Yeah! What do you want to know for?" I said with a smile, "I am looking for a group who would like to know the answers to life's three big questions: Where did we come from, Why are we here, and Where are we going." I could always count on one pointing down and saying, "I know where I am going!"

With this opening, I then would ask if they would like me to do a chalk-talk. Every group said yes, including the Vice Lords, Nobles, and Dukes.

What I learned during these months gave me insights into the real needs of youth and their families. By the next year, I had confirmed the value of my plan in a program called "Campus Teams," and I was invited to teach it at Wheaton College in a course they called "Basic Youth Conflicts."

A year later I could not go back to that board, because that organization had ceased to exist. I am convinced now that if I had not been reviled, there would be no Basic Youth Conflicts Seminar. Thus, I can truly rejoice and be exceeding glad.

The approach that I used on the streets of Chicago is effective everywhere. While passing through La Paz, Bolivia, I stayed at the home of a missionary. He asked me to do a chalk-talk for his church that evening. I agreed and offered to go out on the streets and invite young people to attend. He seemed reluctant, but I just went out and did it. Excitedly, I told him that everyone I invited said that they would come. He told me: "That is why I did not want you to go out. They are only being polite, but don't expect them to come." That night, they all showed up, including a group of students from a nearby college. The missionary said that he had never seen this response before. The students then invited me to speak at their college, which I did.

I learned very quickly that crowds of enthusiastic alumni attract critics. Some are gracious and helpful. Others may be mean-spirited or unreasonable. Whether the people are gracious or gruff, sincere or sarcastic, the command to rejoice and be exceeding glad still applies.

If the calculations for the projected path of a space shuttle are a fraction of a degree off, the shuttle will totally miss its mark. Critics are skilled at finding those mission-critical errors and publicly pointing them out to us.

Crowds Attracted Critics

One day I received in the mail a publication that contained a write-up about the Seminar. At the beginning of the article, the author acknowledged that he had never attended a Seminar but was drawing his conclusions from the supplementary notes that we gave out after each session.

Those notes never were intended to stand alone. They needed the clarity that came from the sessions. Therefore it was not surprising that the author had drawn conclusions that were inaccurate. The article turned out to be a thirty-five-page attack on every part of the material. Any word or statement that could be misunderstood or put in a wrong light was! I was amazed at the things he said we were teaching—which were usually opposite of the things we actually *were* teaching.

Based on all the work, time, and effort he had put into this document, I assumed that he was interested in pursuing the truth, so I called him on the phone and asked if I could explain the things that I was really teaching.

He listened and seemed to be understanding, so I asked if he would be willing to write another article and correct what he had written. He said, "No, I cannot do that." I asked him, "Why do you say that?" He said, "I am on a limited budget, and I cannot afford it." I asked him what it would cost to send out another mailing, and he told me the amount. I told him that I would be happy to pay for this cost. After our phone call, I wrote out a check and sent it to him, but a corrected article was never written.

During my next January in the Northwoods, I took his thirty-five-page attack and went over the Seminar syllabus, word for word, line by line. Anything that was unclear, I rewrote to make sure that it was not misunderstood. As I discovered words whose meanings could easily be misinterpreted, I replaced them with more precise words, to avoid potential misunderstanding.

When I finished, I called my critic and said, "I want to thank you." He said, "For what?" I said: "I have taken your booklet and totally revised our Seminar textbook. I realized when I got done that I could not have paid anyone to be as thorough as you were in pointing out possible misunderstandings, so I want to thank you for your help." He received my thanks, and as a result of his work, millions of people have received help from a much clearer Seminar textbook. Whatever that critic's intentions were, God allowed it for my good.

A Negative Report With a Positive Outcome

A reporter for a widely circulated Christian magazine did a story about the Seminar as it was first beginning to be held around the nation. The tone of the article was definitely negative. In fact, I am told that certain Christian leaders asked him why he would write such a negative article.

A few weeks later I called the reporter. He seemed rather surprised to hear from me. I began the conversation by saying that there were three reasons why I wanted to thank him for how God had used his article.

First, it had motivated me to make sure that the things I teach are clear and Biblically accurate. Second, it had rallied our Seminar alumni to give amazing encouragement. Third, we had received thousands of dollars in further support of our ministry. All three reasons caused me to rejoice.

Matthew 7 gives three tests that determine the validity and stability of a ministry:

1. Floods to test the foundation on which a ministry is built.

2. Torrents of rains to test the spiritual maturity of the leadership.

3. Violent winds that test the constitution of those who made the house.

God promises: "No weapon that is formed against thee shall prosper; and every tongue that shall rise against thee in judgment thou shalt condemn. This is the heritage of the servants of the Lord" (Isaiah 54:17). Noah condemned all of his critics by simply finishing the tasks that God gave him to do.

We are in a war for truth. Thus, we are in enemy territory. If no one is attacking us, it means that we are not a threat to the enemy. Thus, Jesus warned, "Woe unto you, when all men shall speak well of you! for so did their fathers to the false prophets" (Luke 6:26).

Destroying Enemy Strongholds

The most exciting time to rejoice for being reviled is when it is the result of exposing and destroying enemy strongholds.

A stronghold is a false idea or presupposition by which people make unwise decisions. Then they suffer from the resulting pain of guilt, depression, anger, bitterness, and other stresses.

Believers are not only commissioned by God to search out and destroy these strongholds, but we are also given powerful weapons with which to do it: "For the weapons of our warfare are not carnal, but mighty through God to the pulling down of strong holds" (II Corinthians 10:4).

I realized early in my youth that I was in a war for truth, because it is truth that sets people free. Therefore, I knew that I must examine each idea and presupposition and bring it into conformity to the truth that Christ taught in His commands. When a believer comes to the truth, he is free to love the Lord with all his heart, soul, mind, and strength.

Jesus describes Satan as a liar, the father of lies, and one in whom there is no truth. (See John 8:44.) Satan's strongholds are the lies that people believe. Our job is to tear down his strongholds and free all those who are in bondage to him. This brings rewards that will last throughout eternity.

The Power of One Accord

As a result of being reviled for suggesting an order of worship in a church service based on Acts 2:42, I carried out a study that resulted in one of the most important and exciting truths that I have ever seen! It is transforming thousands of lives and freeing them from the bondage of sin. It is the power of being in one accord.

In the first-century Church, God imparted a special power to the believers when they were all in one accord and in one place. (See Acts 2:1–2, 4:24–31, 5:12.) In 2007 we began a program for youth called a Journey to the Heart. It is a ten-day experience in which young people learn how to love God with all of their heart, soul, mind, and strength.

A Journey to the Heart begins at IBLP Headquarters and then travels to the beautiful 3,000-acre Northwoods campus to experience the presence and power of God.

The literal meaning of "one accord" is "the same passion." When a team of ten people all have this love for the Lord, they experience the power of God in a way that they never thought possible!

The Destructive Power of Secret Sin

We explain to the teams at the beginning of the Journey that just as Achan broke the power of God in the armies of Israel with his secret sin (see Joshua 7), similarly if one person on a team has secret sin, the one-accord power of the entire group can be broken. This has encouraged all of them to clear up anything in their life that would hinder God's power!

The newest application of this truth is the formation of *one-accord power teams* of dads. Through once-a-week training times, fathers are equipped to be mighty men of wisdom and success. More details about this outreach are at www.iblp.org/oneaccordteams.

About two thousand young people have gone on a Journey to the Heart. For more information on the Journey, visit www.iblp.org/journey.

The word *power* in the Greek is *dunamis*. English derivatives from this root word include the words *dynamic* and *dynamite*.

In the Westminster Confession of 1646, the authors affirmed the teachings that were universally held as God's truth. On the matter of grace, they wrote, "When God converts a sinner and translates him into the state of grace, He freeth him from his natural bondage under sin; and, by his grace alone, **enables him freely to will and to do** that which is spiritually good." (Westminster Confession of Faith, Chapter IX, "Of free will")

Enjoying God's Power

God desires all believers to experience "the exceeding greatness of his power to us-ward who believe, according to the working of his mighty power" (Ephesians 1:19).

The Power of God's Grace

I begin the Basic Seminar by explaining that one of the most important words in the Bible is *grace*. I point out that *grace* is normally defined as "God's unmerited favor." This is true. However, people can interpret "favor" as either an attitude that God has toward us when we sin or as the divine enablement of God to keep us from sinning.

Based on Scripture, we define *grace* as "the desire and the power that God gives us to do His will." Grace is free. It is given to all people. However, it can be resisted. Those who lived under the law of Moses did not have the power to keep that law, nor did they fully understand its intent. Thus, John wrote, "The law was given by Moses, but **grace** and truth came by Jesus Christ" (John 1:17).

Paul further explained: "If by one man's offense death reigned by one; much more they which receive abundance of **grace** and of the gift of righteousness shall reign in life . . . . That as sin hath reigned unto death, even so might **grace** reign . . . . For sin shall not have dominion over you: for ye are not under the law, but under **grace**" (Romans 5:17, 21; 6:14).

The word *reign* in the Greek is *basileuo*. It means "to be the king, to rule over," and "to have authority and power." The word *dominion* has the same meaning.

The vital importance of equating grace with power is indicated by the vehement attacks that have come to me at the hand of those who insist that grace is simply an attitude with no power.

One Saturday morning I was driving to a neighboring town. At a busy intersection, my 1972 car suddenly stopped. This had never happened before, nor has it happened since!

As cars lined up behind me, I looked across the street and saw two young men come out of a restaurant and run toward me.

Suddenly I realized that they were two fellows on my staff. They had recognized my car and saw that I needed help. They pushed my car into a parking space off the road.

When I got out of the car, a man was standing there asking, "Do you need some help?" I looked at him in amazement. Here was the man who had written so many criticisms of the message I was sharing—especially criticisms of my definition of *grace*.

I said, "Yes, I need a ride back to my office." He agreed to take me. After a few moments of silence, I said, "Only God could have arranged this meeting." He agreed, and we decided to meet in order to try to resolve our differences about what I was teaching.

We met three times, and each time the topic was the definition of *grace*. He did his very best to try to convince me that grace was simply an attitude. As a result, I made a thorough study of every verse in the New Testament that mentions grace. The result was a book, *The Exceeding Great Power of God's Grace*. It has been a benefit to many and is the result of being reviled.

This is the scene that I saw on that Saturday morning as I sat at the intersection of Chicago Avenue and Cass Avenue. The circumstances surrounding this event clearly were arranged by God.

It was exciting to see how 121 New Testament references to grace fit into nine categories of God's power. This leaves no doubt that grace is both the desire and the power God freely gives us to do His will.

The Stronghold of Family Size

The myth of overpopulation has deceived nations into believing that the ideal family has just four people.

Overpopulation is a hoax. All of the people in the world could stand within the city limits of Jacksonville, Florida.

From the beginning of time, Satan has carried on a war against the womb. His goal is to destroy Godly generations, and God's goal is to multiply them.

The Power of Loving Children

One day five pastors were on a conference call with me. Their spokesman said, "Bill, we have been supporting your Seminar for several years, but we are going to stop bringing groups if you continue to mention anything about letting God determine the size of your family." I was shocked by their demand! I stated, "I cannot think of a better issue to be reproached for than loving those whom Jesus loves."

God Is a God of Multiplication

When it comes to children, God is a God of multiplication. The first command that He gave to mankind was to "be fruitful, and multiply" (Genesis 1:22). He repeated this command to Noah and his sons after destroying the first civilization, when He told them to "be fruitful, and multiply, and replenish the earth" (Genesis 9:1). The word *replenish* means "to fill up to overflowing." When God called Abraham, He assured him that He would greatly multiply his seed.

God's Purpose for Multiplication

Jim Bob Duggar, his wife Michelle, and their nineteen children are being admired around the world through their many Discovery Health Channel programs. The one accord in their marriage and family is a powerful example of raising up the foundations of many Godly generations.

When God told Abraham that He would multiply his descendants, God explained why He would do it: "In thee shall all families of the earth be blessed" (Genesis 12:3).

Paul reveals that every believer becomes a part of this promise given to Abraham. (See Galatians 3:8.) Through our children we can bless all nations of the world.

God Rewards Those Who Love Children

Dan and Sandy Webster attended a Basic Seminar in 1983, where they heard for the first time that children are a blessing from God rather than a burden: "Lo, children are a heritage of the LORD: and the fruit of the womb is his reward. As arrows are in the hand of a mighty man; so are children of the youth" (Psalm 127:3–4). They decided to overlook the mocking of their friends, and God gave them four more children.

In 1980, Dan was elected to the Florida state legislature. He was in office for twenty-eight years and ran unopposed for the last twenty-four, during which time he became the Speaker of the House and then the Senate Majority Leader. His political opponents respect him so much that they dedicated a room in his honor at the Capitol, and a local highway was named after him.

Dan and Sandy are living examples of God's promise to those who love children: "They shall not be ashamed, but they shall speak with the enemies in the gate [place of official business]" (Psalm 127:5).

Jordan and Elizabeth Webster would not be in the world today if their parents had not experienced a changed attitude.

A Personal Reason to Love Children

I have had the joy of meeting hundreds of "reversal children," as well as their very grateful parents. One day my mother told me a family secret.

When she conceived me in 1934, America was recovering from the Great Depression. Someone said to her, "How can you afford to have another child?!" She replied, "What should I do about it?" He said, "I know a doctor who will do an abortion." Thus, I am very grateful that my mother had a love for children that was stronger than concern over finances. If she had listened to that friend, I would not be in the world today, and you would not be reading this book.

Libby's parents had a reversal, and God gave them Libby. She has been a great blessing to the Headquarters staff since 2008.

If unwise counsel had been followed, I would not be here.

When God sends rain and sunshine to a given area, He does not determine who receives it based on their spiritual condition. He gives it to the just and the unjust alike. To be perfect, we must do the same thing with our greetings. (See Matthew 5:45–48.)

When we meet anyone, we should imagine what kind of greeting we would give him if he were a very special friend whom we had not seen for a long time. This same quality of greeting should be given to everyone we meet. The results of doing this are amazing.

The Power of "Perfect" Greetings

One of the most common forms of reviling that has come not only to me but also to many others who are seeking to live Godly lives is terms of ridicule such as "legalistic," "holier than thou," or even "cultish."

Our natural response to these and other untrue characterizations is to either turn inward and shut out those whom we know are falsely accusing us or react to them with argumentation and rejection.

It is true that we are to stand alone for truth and that the ability to stand alone comes from the confidence that we have a superior way of life. However, standing alone does not mean cutting ourselves off from other people or looking down on them because they do not measure up to the standards that we believe are right.

While studying Matthew 5:48, I discovered a command of Christ which, if violated, could provoke others to strongly react to us.

A Possible Reason for Being Reviled

Jesus says, "Be ye therefore perfect." To make matters worse, He goes on to say, "Even as your Father which is in heaven is perfect" (Matthew 5:48).

Most of us would exclaim, "But no one is perfect!" However, the context explains the way in which we should be perfect. The previous verse reveals that it is a reference to the way that we greet people whom we meet on a day-to-day basis. (See Matthew 5:47.) We normally brighten up when we meet someone we know, but with strangers our facial responses can communicate the idea that we are not really interested in who they are.

Why This Command Works

Most people do not accept themselves as God designed them, and they fear that others will reject them also. If they see us looking at them with no expression of delight or approval, they immediately will assume that we are rejecting or judging them. In self-defense, they will put up a wall to block us out. If we then try to talk with them about spiritual things, they will think or say, "I saw the way you looked at me, and I am not interested in you or what you have to say."

The word *salute* in Matthew 5:47 means "to embrace someone in the arms of your heart." This must happen at the split second we make eye contact with a person. When I understood this command and began to put it into practice, it transformed my attitude toward people and their responses to me. After I give a perfect greeting, strangers often say, "Do I know you?"

This expression communicates no excitement or delight in the one he is looking at, and he probably would receive a similar response from the other person.

This wholesome smile communicates the right message. It must be ready when eye contact is made.

The Results of a Perfect Greeting

One sunny afternoon I took a group of staff members to a picnic area for a meeting. I spotted a group of empty tables. However, a motorcyclist was sitting at one of them.

I purposed to overlook all of his outward symbols of a different lifestyle and give him a "perfect" greeting. I approached him with a warm smile and enthusiastically said: "Hi! My name is Bill! What is your name?"

He replied, "My name is 'Uncle Mike.' " I said: "I am really happy to meet you, Uncle Mike! We will be using these picnic tables for a little meeting, but I don't want you to feel that you must leave. In fact,

My natural response to those who have a different lifestyle is to pray for God to bless them with His love and truth but not make any special effort to give them a "perfect" greeting.

89

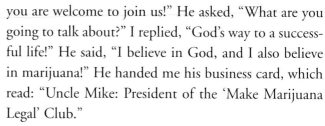

This is the booklet that I gave to "Uncle Mike." It explains how we are not a body with a soul and spirit but rather a spirit in a body with a soul. Uncle Mike was so impressed with this message that he took the book over to two other motorcyclists and explained it to them. Then they wanted copies for themselves. This was the result of giving a "perfect greeting."

When I met "Uncle Mike" in the picnic grove setting, he became my "missionary" to his friends, whom he knew also needed the message that was given to him.

you are welcome to join us!" He asked, "What are you going to talk about?" I replied, "God's way to a successful life!" He said, "I believe in God, and I also believe in marijuana!" He handed me his business card, which read: "Uncle Mike: President of the 'Make Marijuana Legal' Club."

I began signing a booklet as I said: "Uncle Mike, I used to think that I was just a body that had a spirit and soul. Then one day I learned that I am a spirit in a body that also has a soul. This booklet explains what happened in the Garden of Eden. God said to Adam, 'In the day you eat of this tree, you shall surely die.' But Satan said to Eve, 'You will not surely die.'

"God was referring to the spirit of Adam, which died the day he disobeyed. Satan was referring to his body and soul, which lived on for a time. The problem is that Adam's sin was passed on to all of us. Therefore, you and I and all of us are born spiritually dead. The only way to become alive is to be 'born again' through believing in the Lord Jesus Christ."

I handed him the book, which he began reading. Soon two more motorcyclists roared up and went to a nearby picnic table. Uncle Mike walked over and began talking with them. When he left, we waved to each other, and he said, "I'll keep in touch with you, Bill." Later, as we returned to our vans, one of the other motorcyclists came over to me and said, "Could we have one of those books you gave to Mike?"

Several months later I received a call from Uncle Mike. He said: "Bill, I am in trouble with the law. Could I come out and talk to you?" During our talk Uncle Mike and I knelt, and with tears of repentance, Mike received Christ as his Savior.

The Power of One-Accord Marriages

One of the most vicious revilings I have received was carried out in response to a booklet that I wrote in an attempt to prevent the disastrous moral defeats that occur as a result of dating.

I counted more than ninety false or misleading statements in this vitriolic attack, which motivated me to write a more complete book that would explain the foundational principles of a successful marriage. In the process, I discovered a revolutionary approach to marriage that has a solid Biblical base.

The Root Cause of Conflicts

Over the years, I have counseled thousands of married couples. Each time a conflict is described, I can trace it back to fears such as a fear of rejection, a fear of failure, or a fear of lacking future provision.

For example, a wife who fears abandonment would get a job to become self-sufficient. Her husband would fear failure, so he would make his job his main priority and fail to listen to his wife. She then would find a man at work who would listen to her, and she would become emotionally or physically involved with him.

I also found that every fear was based on lies that each person believed about himself or herself, such as "I am not important," "I am not attractive," "I will never be successful," or "I am not worthy to be loved."

These fears and lies often have led to unwise and damaging decisions. The consequences become painful memories. If a husband or wife triggers the return of a painful memory, there usually is an immediate strong reaction by the other partner. This causes another reaction, which only deepens the conflict.

Establishing Biblical Standards of Courtship

An all-out attack was made on this pamphlet. The reviler gave the absurd counsel that a "broken heart of the sort that has a teenager sobbing into his or her pillow one day but heals into hope the next is a natural phase of life." Any successful counselor will acknowledge the long-lasting damage that comes from broken relationships.

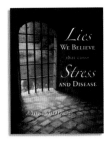

Every painful experience is stored in the limbic system of our brain, which attaches an emotion to it. Whenever this memory is recalled, it will upset the hormonal balance, which leads to sickness and disease.

At most weddings, there are actually six people at the altar. There is the fellow she thinks that he is, the fellow he thinks that he is, and the fellow he really is. The same three are on the girl's side. After marriage, four of them vanish! The goal of courtship is to narrow it down to two people before marriage.

This book provides a foundation for a one-accord marriage. This means that both partners love the Lord with all of their heart, soul, mind, and strength and then allow God to love the other person through them.

I have concluded that there is no way for a couple to have a truly successful marriage unless all these lies, fears, and painful memories are resolved. The best time for this to take place is before marriage.

The new book titled *Seven Courtship Secrets for a Successful Marriage* trains a young man how to help his bride-to-be clear up these lies, fears, and painful memories before the wedding. He then would be doing for her what Jesus is now doing for His Bride, the Church: "That he might sanctify and cleanse it with the washing of water by the word, That he might **present it to himself** a glorious church, not having spot, or wrinkle, or any such thing; but that it should be holy and without blemish" (Ephesians 5:26–28).

One of my greatest sorrows is to watch marriages collapse and families be destroyed. Now that I have this new approach, I will be able to sit down with young men and show them the questions that a prospective father-in-law should ask them so that they can be motivated to live a life with high moral standards.

I then will explain how they can use this and other resources to clear up all of their stresses before marriage. By doing this, I will have the joy of achieving in a greater way my life purpose of helping youth and their families make wise decisions. Millions of strong families and marriages will produce and strengthen the foundation of our nation.

We have weak nations because we have weak families; we have weak families because we have weak fathers. We have weak fathers because no one has trained them how to be wise, courageous, and loving protectors.

"My Joy and Crown"

I have worked with youth groups for the past sixty years. This has given me the opportunity to watch teenagers grow up, get married, have children, and train up their children. I've attended their weddings and seen their grandchildren and even their great-grandchildren. In some cases, the young people in my present ministry are the grandsons and granddaughters of those in my early youth groups.

Each young person has brought joy to me. However, I never have experienced the delight and excitement that I am now having with my present Headquarters staff. No longer do I bring someone on staff to merely do a job. Their first objective is to love God with all their heart, soul, mind, and strength—with no competing affections.

Their second goal is to learn the powerful commands of Christ so that they can teach them to others. Their third goal is to develop skills in order to advance the Kingdom of God in reaching other nations.

The Power of One Accord

The result of this priority is an awesome oneness of fellowship that allows us to be open and genuine with each other and to watch God work supernaturally as we cry out to Him for special needs.

This is the quality of fellowship and interaction that the Apostle Paul urged his disciples to achieve when he wrote, "Fulfill ye my joy, that ye be likeminded, having the same love, being of one accord, of one mind" (Philippians 2:2).

This book, *49 Secrets of Power for Living*, is one of our primary manuals through which to learn the commands of Christ.

The secret of one-accord power is learning each one of these commands and living them out in our daily decisions and activities.

When someone on our staff applies a command and experiences thrilling results from it, he or she shares it as a testimony with the entire group and then uses it to teach others the commands of Christ.

For a free daily commentary on the commands of Christ, visit: www.dailysuccess.org.

Pictured above is a portion of the Headquarters staff in 2009. Most of them first attended a Journey to the Heart, where they learned how to love God with all of their heart, soul, mind, and strength. Each one has an exciting story of God's working in his or her life and how He continues to direct them through the principles of His Word.

The Institute Headquarters in Oak Brook, Illinois, where the staff pictured above serves and receives training

When delegations from other nations visit the Oak Brook Headquarters, they are immediately impressed with the spirit of joy, love, and enthusiasm that they sense from the staff. This causes them to want these students to come to their nation and to train their young people how to be like them.

I can truly say of each one of these staff members what Paul said of those whom he laid down his life to serve: "They are 'my' joy and crown." (See Philippians 4:1.)